Studying creative w

Edited by
Sharon Norris

Imprint information and credits

ISBN: 978-1-907076-43-5(Paperback edition)
978-1-907076-398 (ePub edition)
978-1-907076-404 (PDF edition)

Published under the Creative Writing Studies imprint by
The Professional and Higher Partnership Ltd
Registered office: Suite 7, Lyndon House, 8 King's Court,
Willie Snaith Road, Newmarket, Suffolk, CB8 7SG, UK

Imprint website: creativewritingstudies.wordpress.com
Company website: http://pandhp.com

First published 2013, paperback edition 2014
© Sharon Norris and contributors

Sharon Norris and the contributors assert their rights in accordance with the Copyright, Designs and Patents Act 1988.

This publication is in copyright. Subject to statutory exception and to the provisions of relevant collective licensing agreements, no reproduction of any part may take place without the written permission of The Professional and Higher Partnership Ltd.

Credits
Coverimage:RikaNewcombe(www.rikanewcombe.co.uk)
Cover and text design: Benn Linfield (www.bennlinfield.com)
Editorial and typesetting: Out of House Publishing (www.oohpublishing.co.uk)

Disclaimer

The Professional and Higher Partnership Ltd has no responsibility for the persistence or accuracy of URLs for external or third-party websites referred to in this publication, and does not guarantee that any content on such websites is, or will remain, accurate or appropriate.

The material contained in this publication is provided in good faith as general guidance. The advice and strategies contained herein may not be suitable for every situation. No liability can be accepted by the Professional and Higher Partnership Ltd for any liability, loss, risk, or damage which is incurred as a consequence, whether direct or indirect, of using or applying any of the contents of this book or the advice or guidance contained therein.

The publisher and the author make no warranties or representations with respect to the completeness or accuracy of the contents of this work and specifically disclaim all warranties, including without limitation warranties of fitness for a particular purpose. No warranty may be created or extended by sales or promotional materials.

Series information

Studying creative writing is the fourth title to be published in the international series, Creative Writing Studies. The series comprises titles on creative writing designed for use – by scholars, students, and teachers – in higher education settings.

The first three titles in the series are:

Rethinking creative writing in higher education by Stephanie Vanderslice

Teaching creative writing: practical approaches edited by Elaine Walker

Creative writing: writers on writing edited by Amal Chatterjee

Further titles commissioned for the series include: *Researching creative writing* by Jen Webb.

Contents

vii   Editor's preface

1   Chapter One:
What to expect of a creative writing degree
SHARON NORRIS

7   Chapter Two:
The skills you'll need to study creative writing
ALLY CHISHOLM

20   Chapter Three:
The importance of reading to your writing
SHAWN SHIFLETT

37   Chapter Four:
Pre-writing: how to use journals, notes and plans to improve your writing
LORNA FERGUSSON

55   Chapter Five:
Workshops: what they are (and aren't) and how to make the most of them
JENNIFER YOUNG

71   Chapter Six:
Online learning and how it can help your work
ELIZABETH REEDER

87	Chapter Seven: The role of editing and redrafting, and how to do both SPENCER JORDAN
105	Chapter Eight: Reading aloud: making the most of your work when you present it NABILA JAMEEL
124	Chapter Nine: The role of critical reflections and how to write them SHARON NORRIS
144	Chapter Ten: Assessment: how it's done and its implications for your work HELEN KIDD
165	Chapter Eleven: What happens next? How to proceed after graduation SALLY O'REILLY
182	About the contributors
185	Bibliography
189	Index

Editor's preface

This book is aimed at prospective students, considering taking a degree in creative writing, and existing creative writing students who wish to maximise the benefits of their degree course. Although it's aimed primarily at undergraduate and prospective undergraduate students, increasing numbers of students are taking master's courses in creative writing with no previous experience of studying the subject at undergraduate level. Some of these students may have a degree in a completely unrelated subject such as engineering or medicine; others will have no undergraduate degree at all. For these students and for prospective students who don't know what to expect of a creative writing degree course, this book is intended to help demystify the study of creative writing at university level.

The book is designed to be of interest too to those who teach creative writing at higher education level. All of the contributors have experience of creative writing in higher education: many of us have taught the subject in different countries across the globe. Each of the chapters is based on our own experience, as teachers and as writers.

SHARON NORRIS

Chapter One

What to expect of a creative writing degree

Sharon Norris

If you've recently applied to study creative writing at university, or if you're already a creative writing student, this book aims to help you maximise the benefits of your degree course both by demonstrating how creative writing 'works' within the higher education context and how to take the skills you gain, from editing and pre-writing to the wider 'life-lessons' outlined below, on into life after university. After reading this book we trust that you will also be clearer as to why the things you'll cover again and again on your degree course, such as redrafting, are so important.

The topics covered here are the ones that students either struggle with the most or ask the most questions about or the ones that experience has told the book's contributors are the areas students most need to work on or learn more about. However, there are several chapters, including Shawn Shiflett's on how reading improves creative writing skills, that offer an angle on certain aspects of studying creative writing which you may not have encountered before, as well as others, such as Nabila Jameel's on performing your work, that cover topics rarely touched on in most existing books on studying creative writing.

The book is loosely chronological. It starts with Ally Chisholm's perspective on the skills you'll need to study creative writing and ends with Sally O'Reilly's on life after graduation. In between, the contributors offer their suggestions as to how to approach the various elements that are common to most creative writing degree courses (assessment, the writing workshop and critical reflections). Other chapters, such as Spencer Jordan's guide to effective editing and Lorna Fergusson's on how to use pre-writing to develop work, have a more universal applicability to writers whether at university or not. We want this to be a book you use regularly not just one that sits unused on your bookshelf or computer.

Why study creative writing in a time of uncertainty?

After a period of major expansion during which increasing numbers of 'hands-on' subjects, from dance to photography, and ceramics to creative writing, became part of the university syllabus, there are signs that the higher education sector in many countries is set to contract. In an age of uncertainty, why study creative writing of all subjects?

The benefits of a creative writing degree

The contributors to this book, who (as you'll see from the section 'About the contributors') collectively have a wealth of experience as creative writers in higher education, offer a variety of answers. Sally O'Reilly, who wrote the final chapter, recognises not only the challenges facing soon-to-be-graduating creative writing students but also the potential advantages they possess. The ability to organise material, excellent and accurate writing skills and attention to detail in editing and presenting are all highly marketable in an increasingly competitive job market. So too is the ability to follow through with ideas, a central focus of Lorna Fergusson's chapter on pre-writing.

In one sense, aside from the specific skills taught and developed on a creative writing degree, it fulfils the same role that a degree in any arts or humanities subject did in the past: a way of training and disciplining the mind, a forum for developing a range of transferable skills and a useful introduction to academia for anyone who wishes to continue their studies at a higher level.

Creative writing degrees, however, also offer something more: a unique opportunity for self-discovery and development. In my own chapter on critical reflections, I make the point that writing is, by its very nature, a reflective activity. Finding out who you are, what you think and what matters to you is a fundamental part of life, and creative writing students have the freedom to explore these issues through their writing over an extended period. I don't know if any research has been done on whether creative writing graduates are 'better adjusted' on leaving university than students who take any other degree course, but it remains one of the few subjects in higher education where there is still (considerable) room for self-exploration, not just 'training for employment'. Furthermore, virtually every chapter here, implicitly or explicitly, highlights the unique role of creative writing degrees in helping to develop the imagination.

All of which is not to say that creative writing graduates don't leave university with an array of practical skills that would be attractive to potential employers. In addition to those mentioned above, Elizabeth Reeder's chapter demonstrates not only that the online environment can aid in the development of writing skills but also that writing skills can help to develop our effectiveness in the range of online environments that we now inhabit or participate in. Nabila Jameel, in her chapter on reading and presenting work aloud, also points to the potential benefits and applications of the skills gained from learning to read and perform creative work to a live audience.

Both Shawn Shiflett and Ally Chisholm in their chapters point to an additional and crucial skill that creative writing degrees help to develop: the ability to use a range of 'outside' sources and stimuli, to distil these in the imagination and to apply them to the process of making something new. In cognitive psychology this is the hallmark of the creative mind. It's also an essential quality in business and entrepreneurship.

Ally Chisholm's chapter, however, suggests that studying creative writing also has deeper benefits. In arguing that good research skills are essential for writers, his chapter shows how, through developing our 'hearing' and our awareness of the world around us, we learn to recognise the inauthentic and the superficial.

Both Jennifer Young and Elizabeth Reeder's chapters also point to the wider 'life lessons' to be learned from studying creative writing. Where Elizabeth's explores etiquette in the virtual environment, Jennifer's emphatically drags lone writers from the garret (if they were ever there in the first place) and seats them at the centre of a community of writers in the creative writing workshop, where each member seeks to help and support the other. If, as Jennifer argues, the workshop is at the heart of creative writing studies at university, then in teaching students how to take turns, how to give and receive feedback, how to listen actively and how to offer constructive criticism of the work without undermining the person, it offers crucial lessons for life, not just for the duration of a degree course.

Both Sally O'Reilly's chapter and Helen Kidd's note that most creative writing degrees also offer practical advice to students, especially those in the final year, on how to 'get their work out there'. At the same time, Sally's acknowledges the reality of the situation: over seventy higher education institutions in the UK alone producing a new crop of talented creative writing graduates every year, an increasingly depleted (traditional) publishing industry and a growing e-publishing sector whose benefits for the writer still appear to some to be double-edged.

That said, 't'was ever thus'. The ratio of would-be writers to publishing outlets has always been disproportionate, and when have writers ever not lived in 'an age of uncertainty'? What Sally's chapter ultimately highlights is the fact that creative writing is 'vocational' in the truest sense of the word: you've really got to want to do it. You must be tenacious, and you'll need to be willing to develop an array of skills – from those that are strictly 'writing-based' to the ability to use social networking to publicise yourself.

A creative writing degree offers students the chance to hone and develop these skills over time and a safe place in which to do this. It also offers exposure to professionals who know the market and how to negotiate it and who can help increase the chances of publication by developing awareness of what is good writing (and what isn't). Students also learn how to how to pitch and how to submit manuscripts and to whom.

5

Preparing to study creative writing

If you're not yet studying creative writing at university but have applied, we hope this book will help to prepare you by giving you an idea of what to expect on a creative writing degree course and the areas you'll be focusing on. If you're still not sure whether to apply, we hope the book will provide you with a sense of what's involved, and perhaps also help you to decide which is the best course for you. In the meantime, you can use this book to familiarise yourself with the territory and to practise the skills you'll need to study creative writing.

Chapter Two

The skills you'll need to study creative writing
Ally Chisholm

The previous chapter will have given you a better understanding of what to expect on a creative writing degree course. The purpose of this chapter is to get you thinking, perhaps before you've even chosen the course you want to take, about the sorts of skills you'll need in order to get the most from a creative writing degree. It's important to note from the outset that you won't necessarily need to master every skill listed here. Some of the skills listed are more applicable to those who wish to specialise in journalism, others to poetry, while others still are more relevant to fiction writers. Also, there are elements of writing that some writers are better at than others. Furthermore, not every novel, poem or script is 'built' in the same way. The point is that a good writer should know how they are built and what goes into a poem or novel or screenplay.

A willingness to learn

Perhaps the most important advice to give any first-time student is that you should be open to learning new things. This may sound obvious, and you would hope that all students would come to class with this mindset. But in the case of creative writing courses you are perhaps more likely to meet students who have a passion for writing and who have spent time practising their craft before arriving at university. However, this can lead to writing students believing that they are already writers and that there is nothing more to learn. In which case, why are they studying for a writing degree? No aspiring writer is going to develop their craft if they think they already know everything. The key thing I always tell students is that you don't have to agree with everything you are taught. There should always be room for debate in literary and creative studies. That's part of what being a student is about. But you can't have that debate until you know the facts and are familiar with the theories. For example, a writing student who doesn't read widely might think their work is highly original, when if they'd only done their reading, they would have known that lots of books have been written in that style or published on that topic.

Evening classes and writing groups can give you the opportunity to write and meet other writers. However, a degree provides you with the opportunity to spend three or even four whole years learning and growing.

Learn to read as a writer

The importance of reading cannot be understated and rightly deserves an entire chapter in this book. Suffice to say here that you don't have to be well read before you start your course, but by the time you finish you will have been given every chance to become so. Your department will provide you with a reading list. Your library will provide you with resources, including (in most universities) a subject liaison librarian who will specialise in your area of study. With these opportunities available, the most important aspect of writing is to learn to love reading (if you don't already) and to love storytelling in all its forms. However, I would add to this that you should also learn to enjoy reading theories of writing. I'm sure that for most young writers, reading textbooks about *how* to write doesn't seem as much fun as the actual creative process, but the more you write the more you want to understand how to do it better. You don't have to agree with all the theories you'll read, but you should be aware of how they can help you. The more you begin to understand about the process of writing the better your work will be for it. These books can also help you to become more aware of the fact that everything you write adds to an existing heritage of the written word.

The power of description

Young writers are often preoccupied with coming up with ideas for stories and thinking of subject matter for non-fiction. With this in mind, you might think I'd say that the most important thing for a creative writing student is to be full of ideas. However, many students forget that first of all they need to get to grips with description. You may be very good at coming up with ideas, you may have an incredible awareness of what people want to read, but you'll still need to practise how best to describe what you want to convey.

Writing that's simply a series of events or 'what happened next' and has no detail or description is little more than a synopsis. Being able to write a synopsis is a useful skill in its own right. The point here is that there's a lot more to writing a story or play or poem than coming up with an initial idea. Even non-fiction writers don't simply write a list of events. They describe them. They may research the events and organise them to make the best possible sense of the facts, but good writing, good storytelling in all forms, is about *how* we tell stories.

A writer needs to be able to fill in the details. If you choose to describe a stately home, then you must be able to make this establishment come to life for the reader. How does this specific stately home smell? Does the odour of polished oak linger in the air? What noises can you hear? Is it bustling with servants or can you hear the creak of every floorboard? Even if the reader has been to a hundred stately homes, you want to make sure that they can differentiate the one you are writing about from all the others. If it's a real place and the reader has been there, you want them to be able to recognise it from your writing.

A writer's work is unique because he or she makes their writing specific. If you're a fiction writer, for example, you may be able to think of the greatest storyline ever for a novel, but if you can't make the reader care about your characters, and, crucially, if you cannot describe all the scenes that make the plot move forward, then it's unlikely to be a success. Have you ever jumped in the back of a taxi in, say, London? That's a place where you'll hear a lot of interesting stories, but this doesn't mean that every taxi driver is a writer waiting to be discovered. There is a craft involved in using words in writing, as opposed to other modes of storytelling. It isn't always the best plots that succeed. It is technically possible to write without a plot, but it is virtually impossible to write even the most abstract work without description.

One technique you can use to become a better writer is to try describing a few scenes from particular story ideas you've come up with. You don't need to write like Tolstoy, lavishly describing every single aspect of a scene. There are different levels of description. Another good idea is to practise writing about the most mundane things (going to the shops, walking up your stairs, sitting on a bus), and making them interesting.

Also, be experimental in your reading. Try reading heavily descriptive works *and* the works of minimalist writers. See the different ways scenes can be described. This may also help you to discover whether you are a novelist, playwright, screenwriter or poet. Perhaps you're the sort of person who reads a book and is immediately able to imagine vividly what it would like as a film or sound like as a radio play. Thinking of *how* you want to tell stories is a good starting point. It could also help you choose the type of creative writing degree course that you want to follow (e.g., one that's more general, or one with a strong focus on, say, screenwriting).

But first of all you need to test yourself to see how much you actually like writing. Are you are prepared to advance beyond thinking up ideas for stories and actually start writing?

Memorable use of language

Poetry, in particular, is all about finding the right words, and the enduring popularity of Shakespeare also has a lot to do with his use of language. If we consider the dialogue in a Shakespeare play, we care about *what* is being said and the meaning it has within the wider context of the play, but mostly we remember *the way* it is said. Think about Hamlet's 'To be or not to be' speech. He is questioning whether it is better to live or die, and there are so many ways to say that. But Shakespeare didn't just write, 'Shall I live or die? Wouldn't it be easier to just give up instead of face the troubles of life?' We can debate endlessly what makes writing quotable and memorable (e.g., vivid imagery, choice of vocabulary) but we know instinctively that 'slings and arrows of outrageous fortune' sounds better than 'the troubles of life'. In your own work, try to experiment with finding better ways to say what you want to say. Read your work aloud, whatever genre you're writing in, and listen to how it sounds.

The screenwriter and novelist William Goldman says in his book *Adventures in the screen trade* that there are only a handful of scenes in a film that an audience will remember. They will remember what the story was about and the overall plot, but the quotable moments are the ones that last. Your choice of language gives you the opportunity to make your work memorable. You don't have to use big long words. The writer John Steinbeck, for example, is remembered for his effective use of simple language. Making your language memorable doesn't have to mean using words that will have the reader reaching for the nearest dictionary.

In the introduction to his book, *On writing*, Stephen King notes that readers often overlook the fact that even horror writers care about the language they use. It is often assumed that all genre fiction is plot-driven, while literary fiction relies on beautiful language to be successful. The truth is that all writers use language and want their language to be memorable. Some just use it better than others, and some produce more quotable work than others.

While it is easy to become fixated on plot and ideas, perhaps the best thing to come to class with is a love of words. In preparation, think about what you find most quotable in your favourite pieces of writing and why. Again, this could help you choose your course and decide what kind of writing you're best suited to.

The ability to organise your ideas

Planning and structuring are essential skills for any kind of writing. Consider your descriptive work and your use of language as the 'bricks and mortar' of your writing. Once you have these, you'll need to think about what you want to build with those bricks.

Many writers believe that good writing doesn't need a plot. It is true that some works simply show us a world that we visit and explore while reading yet where perhaps very little happens. Even in these cases there's always a plan, a structure. A good example is the Bret Easton Ellis's novel *American psycho*. If you were to describe the 'plot' of this novel you could say only that it is a book about a man who kills a lot of people, with each murder more gruesome than the last. He is not pursued. He is not caught. He is not remorseful by the end. We do get an insight into the horrible world of the psychopath and we do feel we have been on a journey, but how would we describe the plot?

If we define 'plot' as everything that happens then, as not much happens in the novel, we could say there isn't much in the way of plot. But there is definitely a structure. If there wasn't, the order in which Ellis has events happen wouldn't matter. Why not start a book called *American psycho* with a murder? Why does it take until more than a hundred pages for the first murder to occur? However, the author is building to something. He is pacing. He is stirring an emotional response in the reader. Plot is *what* happens. Structure is *how* it happens, the order in which it happens, and the appropriate place for every scene.

If you are a confident writer, it's easy to believe that everyone will be bowled over by your elegant prose, your cleverly thought out scenes and captivating dialogue. However, sometimes even these things still aren't enough. Even if you believe that plot is relatively unimportant, you do have to understand that structure is essential. I challenge anyone to pick up a book or watch a film or play that they regard as having little in the way of plot and see no structure in it.

There are many books about how to structure your writing, such as David Mamet's *A whore's profession* and Rob McKee's *Story*. Both express the idea that every scene has or should have a purpose and every scene ends when it reaches that purpose. There is an art to making the reader want to keep on reading. On a creative writing degree, you will learn to plan, but having a plan is not the same as knowing how your writing will conclude. You may not know the ending. Or you may think you know it, but it changes and it could change again before you reach the last scene. But you should be able to set out with a road map of where you want to go and the sights you want your reader to see along the way if you learn to structure.

Some writers write extensive plans, and it's standard for non-fiction writers to submit lengthy proposals (which in themselves need planning) to agents and publishers. Some fiction authors claim to have no written plan at all, but even they have some sort of plan in mind. They have a starting point and ideas about where they want to go and where they could possibly end. No writer is ever completely without a plan. As a writer, I always have a distinct idea where I'm starting and where I want my protagonists to go. I know a series of events that I want to write and I know the logical order for them to go in. All of this is written down in a plan that I can consult as I go along. Pieces of plot and dialogue regularly get added and moved around. I don't know how I'd retain all this information and keep track of the shape of my work without it.

Lots of ideas

Even if having lots of ideas is not enough in itself to make you a good writer, it does help. What's the point in having great organisational skills if you have nothing to organise? You should be a compulsive note-taker, stockpiling scenes and ideas. You may not use every single one, but at least you will have them in reserve. Never throw away even the ideas that you think are not that good. A discarded short story could provide the inspiration for, or form the bones of, longer pieces of work. An incomplete poem could become a great monologue. Ideas for one novel that never seemed to work out could provide a backstory or subplot to the next one. I find that when I have many ideas and scenes and snippets of dialogue and well-described locations, then concepts for stories and poems are easier to come by.

Good research skills

Gathering, investigating and assessing material is important in any job, and research adds authority and believability to any kind of writing. Non-fiction writers can find their reputations discredited by inaccuracies. However, you may think that in fiction, where the writer creates his own world with its own rules, that there is no need for research. But fiction is dependent on creating a literary world that we can all relate to, one that has a resounding familiarity. In other words, we want our audience to be able to relate to the work.

I was once given a short story to read that was set in an American diner. It had interesting characters with interesting issues and the dialogue was sharp. The scene was well described. Yet I didn't find it engaging at all. The biggest problem was that the setting matched every diner scene I'd seen in every small independent American film and all the characters were young, 'cool' and messed up on drugs. The writer's voice lacked authority because it seemed like someone else's idea of an American diner. No real research had been done. I had no sense that this writer knew the world he was writing about. It quickly becomes clear to the reader when you're guessing what something is like. Your work seems the weaker for it.

Research also makes your study more enjoyable and allows you to become more involved in the world you're creating. It can even give you a better insight into your own work. Everything and anything can be research to a writing student. For my own creative writing master's dissertation, I had written a novel in which the protagonist had studied Russian history. I knew why the character had done so. What I didn't know was anything at all about Russian history! The only way to get around that was to research the subject. Not only did I enjoy doing this, I also understood my protagonist better. I started to think of reasons why Russian history and literature would appeal to him, and, as a result, I could make him seem more believable as a person. Researching the background to my novel in this way made me feel more involved with the work. It made me think about it in new ways and, in turn, I was able to incorporate my research into the work. Ultimately, the research provided me with more ideas and more to write about.

Attention to detail

Literary agents and publishers often say they can tell from looking at just one page of a manuscript whether or not it is a publishable piece of work. This idea is alarming, especially if you've spent months or years completing and rewriting your 100,000-word manuscript.

Even as a writing student, your aim should be to produce work that looks professional. Your course will demand it and your tutors will want you to adopt good habits that you can nurture throughout and beyond your degree course. You will need to demonstrate that you have taken time and care over your writing. You should always use the spell-check facility on your computer, but don't rely on spell-check alone as it does not catch every grammatical error. Sloppy spelling not only doesn't look good but your tutors will also want to see that you are aware of, and have adhered to, industry standard. Proofreading shouldn't just be left to editors.

Similarly, page layout is an integral part of writing and not an afterthought. Layout can influence the pacing of a piece of writing. Pauses and blank spaces are important. This is perhaps most evident in poetry. If you were to try to imagine a poem, any poem, on a printed page, it wouldn't look like a novel. But whether you're writing poetry, novels or plays, you always need to be aware of layout. If you don't believe me, try reading a page of text that's one solid block of words, with no paragraph breaks. It can be tiring. That's not to say that you can't write a solid block of text if you want to. You wouldn't be the first to do so. But you should be aware that the way your text looks on paper could affect how it is read and, potentially, an agent or publisher's willingness to pick it up.

Conclusion: have as many strings to your bow as possible and be open to new ideas

The desire to learn more about writing should drive your desire to study. If you already have a love of the written word and of stories, whether they're told in fiction or non-fiction, poetry or prose, then you'll want to learn more about them. You can take issue with the order in which I've listed the skills I've referred to here, and you yourself may put more emphasis on some than on others, but ignore any of them, and you'll be at a disadvantage.

While it's true that some writers are better at certain aspects of writing than others and while there are particular skills required of the journalist or the novelist, writing is writing and you need to be open to all forms. Also, while I've emphasised here how the skills I have listed can help you become a better writing student and, in the long run, a better writer, these same skills (how to research, attention to detail, spelling and layout) can be used throughout your life and in many different employment situations.

Having read over the list of skills above one final time, I'm aware that much of what I've said sounds obvious, but it can be easy to forget and to take certain aspects of writing for granted. There is so much to learn about writing and there are many questions you will want to ask. But before you even think up those questions, you should ask yourself if you can do the basics. If you can, then you have good foundations on which to build.

Chapter Three

The importance of reading to your writing

Shawn Shiflett

Writers read differently to other readers

On the surface, writers read novels, short stories, memoirs, poems, creative non-fiction essays and other forms of writing for the same reason most readers do: we get a kick out it. Certainly, reading also quenches your thirst for a greater understanding about the human condition, educates you as to the differences and universalities of cultures and gives you an endless stream of intellectual food for thought. All of that good stuff aside, we first and foremost read a piece of writing simply for the dramatic, seeing-in-the-mind pleasure of it. Reading takes us *out* of ourselves and, paradoxically, *into* ourselves as well.

We have all felt so physically transported from the words on a page to the world they bring to three-dimensional life in the theatre of our minds, that hours, days, weeks or even years after we've put the piece of writing back onto our bookshelf we will find ourselves once again mentally revisiting images from it. For example, if I hear someone mention Leo Tolstoy's epic novel *War and peace*, I immediately think of Prince André lying mortally wounded on the battlefield as he stares up at the 'immeasurably lofty' sky (Tolstoy, *War and peace*, p. 326). And once, while seated on a commuter train, I suddenly felt as if I were in a small boat that was rocking to the dip and roll of swells on the open Atlantic. Stranger still, the train was at a complete stop at a station. I realised that my visceral sensation of sailing was coming from none other than Virginia Woolf's *To the lighthouse*, a novel I had finished reading a few hours earlier.

As it is such a common experience, perhaps we could agree henceforth to classify such occurrences as 'post-*dramatic* flashbacks'.

When you finish reading a compelling story, you will often feel a strong need to share with others how you liked one character, loathed another, felt sorry for a third and will absolutely never forgive a fourth. You may have found yourself trying telepathically to influence a character's bad choices into good ones, momentarily forgetting that the person of concern to you is but an imaginative collection of made-up details. Dwell too hard on why a protagonist did not adhere to your brand of common sense and you might even daydream about giving that individual a piece of advice. In short, the more an author succeeds in pulling you hook, line and sinker into the world created by his or her prose, the greater your emotional investment in the people who inhabit that world.

You may be thinking, 'True enough, but I occasionally stop to admire the artful language of a given phrase, piece of dialogue, image, as well as other aspects of an author's style.' (Note: in this chapter, I will also refer to style as *voice*, though I know that the two terms are not strictly one and the same.) This is all well and good, but do you feel as if you are reading in a manner that gives you much more than a rudimentary insight into the complexities of an author's craft on the page? Probably not. To accomplish that, you need to develop the ability to have a *second* reading experience, one that parallels your first, more intimate and enjoyable experience but also maintains a safe distance from the seductive power of the story.

This is not to imply that you can no longer read just for the pleasure of it. That would be a crime. Rather, you must learn how to read with an analytical eye that observes and dissects the craft of writing in order to 'borrow' skills from other writers that are of use to you in your own writing. Think of someone studying the art of magic, who enjoys being fooled by a master magician's performance of an illusion but who immediately after witnessing it wants to learn the secret set of skills behind it. Only then will the student be able to attempt the trick himself and hopefully pull the wool over the eyes of the audience too. In the same way, a writer reads to learn the craft and process of writing, and thinking about these specific objectives as you read is an essential tool you can use to develop your own unique voice.

A list of questions

The novelist William Faulkner famously advised writers to read everything they could, whether it was good or bad. One way you can use reading to improve your writing is to ask yourself what attracts you about an author's voice. Then, using your curiosity as a guide, write a list of questions. You will have to go further than simply reflecting on what you liked or disliked about a character, the general plot line of a story, how the prose was too graphic or too tame for your taste, etc. Instead, keep your attention on the things in the writing that make you want to ask, 'How did the author do that?'

Below is a list of sample questions I drew up. As I am primarily a novelist, I have focused on that form; however, feel free to steal or tailor any of the questions below to your own chosen genre. After all, words and images are just as much a poet's building blocks as they are for the novelist, short story writer, or essayist.

Sample questions

1. What does the first sentence of the novel accomplish for the reader? The first paragraph? First chapter?
2. What do you notice about the way an author ends one chapter and then begins the next?
3. Do you ever hear the author's tone or personality seeping into the prose?
4. In a story told by a first-person narrator, do you ever suspect that the author's opinions about the narrator are completely different to those the narrator holds about himself? If so, how does this 'layering' contrasting of points-of-view help to dramatise the story?
5. How does the author describe a landscape, room or any other type of place and what sights and images does he use (e.g., the quality of light, particular objects, smells, sounds)?
6. How does the author handle the story's timeline and any time jumps within it?
7. Does the author vary the novel's pacing and mood? If so, when and to what effect?
8. How are characters introduced? Is there always an immediate physical description of one when he or she walks onto the story 'stage' for the first time? For the second time? Third? Which characters get more physical description than others?

9. Is the author always careful to make sure that the reader knows where characters are in spatial relation to each other? Does he make sure most of the time? Some of the time? Never?

10. Does the writer ever change point-of-view from one character to another without the use of a page or chapter break? If so, how does he do this without the reader noticing until well after the 'shift' has already occurred? Why does he even change point-of-view and to what effect?

There is no hard-and-fast rule about answering questions in the exact order you wrote them down, but let's go ahead and start with the first one:

1. What does the first sentence of the novel accomplish for the reader? The first paragraph? First chapter?

Gustave Flaubert is generally regarded as one of the fathers of the modern novel, so let's start by seeing what we notice about the first sentence in *Madame Bovary*: 'We were in class when the headmaster came in, followed by a new boy, not wearing the school uniform, and a school servant carrying a large desk' (Flaubert, *Madame Bovary*, p. 5). Not exactly as if there are guns blazing or bombs dropping out of the sky from the novel's get-go, but dwell on this opening sentence for a moment longer. Do you remember what it was like in primary school when a new pupil entered the room? The paragraph ends with this second sentence: 'Those who had been asleep woke up, and everyone rose as if just surprised at his work' (Flaubert, *Madame Bovary*, p. 5).

All eyes are on the boy who turns out to be none other than Charles Bovary, a focusing of everyone's undivided attention that you, like a fellow classmate, join in. Keep in mind, too, that as the novel is titled *Madame Bovary*, you're probably wondering, 'Where is she?' The chapter then goes into a hilarious, if not also humiliating, scene for Charles where he becomes the class scapegoat and brunt of everyone's pranks. Students make fun of his name, slap his hat out of his hands and flip paper pellets from the tips of their pens at him.

Images such as these take many of us back to similar moments in our own childhood school experiences. I can think of times when I was the one being mercilessly teased by classmates, as well as other times where I gladly joined in with the group teasing some other unfortunate soul, trusting in the cruel, short-sighted reasoning of 'better him than me'. Thus, I fully recognise the scene's universal truth from both sides of the bullying fence, which explains why, as a reader, I find myself in an emotional tug-of-war between cringing and laughing out loud. By the end of the opening scene, I am sufficiently empathic with Charles to want to read what comes next – a fast move through time that delves into the backstory of his childhood and ends with the marriage to his first wife, all of which highlights his utter mediocrity.

Had these two sections of writing been reversed in story order, the reader might well put the book down or at the very least wonder why they should care about a character whose greatest attribute is his laziness. As it stands, our original empathy for Charles dilutes our irritation with him enough for us to keep turning pages. I should add here that Flaubert's occasionally snide tone throughout this chapter is highly entertaining. Finally, he gives the reader one last incentive to find out what will become of Charles by bringing Part I to a close with the following foreshadowing:

> When Charles returned in the evening, she [his first wife] stretched forth two long thin arms from beneath the sheets, put them round his neck, and having made him sit down on the edge of the bed, began to talk to him of her troubles: he was neglecting her, he loved another. She had been warned she would be unhappy: and she ended by asking him for a dose of medicine and a little more love.
> (Flaubert, *Madame Bovary*, pp. 13–14)

Obviously, all is not right with Charles Bovary's first marriage, which brings to mind a further question: have you ever read a story where something *doesn't* go wrong with a character sooner rather than later? In other words, we continue reading simply to find out whether or not Charles continues on his hapless, lazy path or finds the wherewithal to get his act together in subsequent chapters. We are also curious to know how an entire novel could possibly be about either of the less-than-flattering Madame Bovaries (Charles's mother and his wife) introduced after the opening classroom scene. However, we need not worry, for Emma Bovary, Charles's second wife, is about to make her grand entrance.

The first sentence of Charles Johnson's novel *Oxherding tale* reads as follows: 'Long ago my father and I were servants at Cripplegate, a cotton plantation in South Carolina' (Johnson, *Oxherding tale*, p. 3). So far, Johnson has set the place and clarified the basic relationship of two characters. The second sentence reads:

> That distant place, the world of my childhood, is ruin now, mere parable, but what history I have begins there in an unrecorded accident before the Civil War, late one evening when my father, George Hawkins, still worked in the Big House, watched over his owner's interests, and often drank with his Master – this was Jonathan Polkinghorn – on the front porch after a heavy meal.
>
> (Johnson, *Oxherding tale*, p. 3)

The words 'accident' and 'unrecorded' have us all ears. The chapter (or more precisely, the scene) that follows the opening preamble becomes an account of how slave and master, under the influence of too much Madeira, decide to swap wives for the night. The end result is that George Hawkins (the slave) impregnates the half-asleep Anna Polkinghorn (the slave master's wife) before she is awake enough to realise that it is not her husband with whom she is having sexual relations. Once she does, she switches from a state of carnal bliss to one that makes her 'let fly with a scream'. She is still 'howling' as George, 'hauling hips outside', runs from the Big House in the direction of the slave's quarters. Up ahead, another woman's scream (this one from George's wife, Mattie) is heard, followed by Jonathan flying 'like a chicken fleeing a hawk' out the front door of the Hawkins's cabin. The scene comes to an uproarious end with the men exchanging a few words as they cross paths, neither one prepared to accept the blame for their marital predicaments. Then, in a closing comment, Andrew Hawkins, the bi-racial narrator of the story, states, 'This, I have been told, was my origin' (Johnson, *Oxherding tale*, p. 7).

The opening chapter to *Oxherding tale* is so weirdly comical (a slave master suggesting to his slave that they should wife swap) that the reader is left fully engaged and ready to continue reading in order to find out how Andrew will ever win his freedom and make a comfortable life for himself in the pre-Civil War Southern states of the USA.

Dorothy Allison's novel *Bastard out of Carolina* begins, 'I've been called Bone all my life, but my name's Ruth Anne' (Allison, *Bastard out of Carolina*, p. 1). Your first question is probably, 'Her name is *what?*' If you want to find out why the narrator is called Bone, you have to read on. She was born shortly after her mother Annie, eight months pregnant, flew through the windshield of a pickup truck during a car accident.

> Mama was just asleep and everyone else was drunk. And what they did was plow headlong into a slow-moving car. The front of Uncle Travis's Chevy accordioned; the back flew up; the aunts and Uncle Travis were squeezed so tight they just bounced a little; and Mama, still asleep [in the back seat] flew right over their heads, through the windshield, and over the car they hit … Of course, she didn't wake up for three days, not till after Granny and Aunt Ruth had signed all the papers and picked out my name.
>
> (Allison, *Bastard*, p. 2)

It is also on page two that we find out that Bone got her nickname when she was brought home from the hospital and her Uncle Earl 'announced' she was 'no bigger than a knucklebone'. Granny had already run Bone's father out of town for getting Annie pregnant, and the opening to the novel concludes with the circumstances that led to the state of South Carolina officially declaring Bone a 'bastard' on her birth certificate (Allison, *Bastard*, pp. 2–3).

The beginning of this novel is similar to the one in *Oxherding tale* in that the narrators of both stories – either not yet born or not old enough to have memories of the events being told – must have got their information second-hand from other family members. A significant difference between the two narrators, however, is that while Johnson has Andrew stick to fleshing out and dramatising one particular scene, Allison has Bone move quickly through a series of events and facts. Remarkably, all of the above information in *Bastard out of Carolina* is compressed into three printed pages that leave you sufficiently curious as to where Bone and her hard-drinking extended family are headed. No-holds-barred tragedy, at times salted with self-deprecating humour, is afoot.

I could go on examining how other novels lift off from the story launch pad, but the underling similarity in these three books is that each of the authors is making sure – subtly or overtly – that the reader has an immediate reason (if not several) to keep reading and to want to find out what happens next. It is as if they are deliberately dropping breadcrumbs intended to whet your story-appetite. Beginnings of novels are, it is often said, one of the hardest parts of that particular narrative form to successfully write, so let us tip our hats to Flaubert, Johnson and Allison and move on.

Making your own list

Here are some more sample questions:

10. How does the author go about developing plot? Are there subplots? If so, how do they feed into the overarching plot? (Keep in mind that different successful novels will lead you to different answers to many of these questions. For example, does *To the lighthouse* have a plot beyond whether or not any of the characters will ever get to that damn lighthouse? One could argue that the richness of Virginia Woolf's prose and the underlying psychological intrigue between characters are more than enough to keep generations of readers engaged and turning pages.)

11. Where does the author 'tease' you, the reader, by foreshadowing events? What images, metaphors, lines of dialogue or other moments in the story does he or she use to achieve foreshadowing? Is foreshadowing happening sometimes without your noticing it on a conscious level?

12. What are the 'big' scenes in the story? What makes them big? Is it just length? And in these scenes, how are (a) descriptive images of *place*, (b) the use of *dialogue*, and (c) *character interaction* being used and shuffled back and forth for dramatic effect? Do any of the story's major scenes fail to use all three? (I will save you some time here, as in general the answer is *no* with the obvious exception of scenes where only one character is present. However, each author has his or her own artful ways of building a major scene, and much can be learned from comparing and contrasting how different writers go about doing it.)

13. In between big scenes, what do smaller scenes and fast moves through time accomplish for the novel's overarching structure?

14. There is the *moment* of story (such as a vivid image) and the *movement* of story through time. Where do you see these two important parts of storytelling working in tandem?
15. Does the author use flashbacks? If so, what is gained or lost by not telling the story in chronological order? How are flashbacks introduced?
16. Why does a particular metaphor stay burned in your memory? If the author had decided to delete it, would anything crucial be lost to the story?
17. What did the last chapter or epilogue accomplish for your overall reading experience?

Now it's your turn. Make your list as long, short, complex or as simple as you like. Don't be intimidated if you can only come up with a few questions to begin with. Often, answering just one question will lead you to ask several new ones. Again, the only rule here is to *follow and trust your curiosity*. Keep reminding yourself of what it is you are after: an exploration of the craft of the particular writing forms that attract you.

What to do with your list

Pull some of your favourite novels off your bookshelves (or a library's bookshelves) and start looking for answers to your questions. The fifth question on my list was 'How does the author handle the story's timeline and the time jumps within it?' It's not a bad idea to start off by going through one or more of your novel choices line by line and marking every instance where the author has given his or her story a nudge, bump, jump or even an all-out

31

sprint forwards or backwards in time. Let's look at *Bastard out of Carolina* once again and examine some of Dorothy Allison's time-management skills on the page.

In Chapter 5, right after a section break, Bone says, 'Daddy Glen [Bone's stepfather] didn't do too well at RC Cola. He kept getting transferred to different routs or having to pay for breakage, and no matter how hard he and Mama worked, there never seemed to be enough money to pay the bills' (Allison, *Bastard*, p. 63).

For those of us who teach using the Story Workshop® method originated and developed by John Schultz, the above 'basic form' is referred to as a 'model telling' (Schultz, *Writing from start to finish*, pp. 120–46).[1] In it, time becomes compressed to show repeated patterns that tell us something about a place, an activity, or a person – in this case about Daddy Glen. The phrase, 'He kept' implies *often*, as does the phrase 'never seemed to be enough money'. Interspersed throughout Bone's detailing of the family's precarious financial circumstances are moments of dialogue where a character said something at a particular time, as in the following example: '"Maybe you better ask James [Glen's brother] for that money he was gonna give you," Mama suggested the day Daddy Glen came home to say he'd been laid off' (Allison, *Bastard*, p. 63).

This remark by Annie begins a 'mini scene' between Annie and Glen that lasts for only about a page in length and consists mostly of dialogue between those two characters. Occasionally, Allison gives readers a particular sight of one of them, such as in the sentence, 'Glen's face seemed to squeeze in on itself as he ran his hands down from his hairline to his neck' (Allison, *Bastard*, p. 63). The reader gets little, if anything, in the way of descriptions to indicate *place* or to define where characters are at a given moment. Then following a section break, Bone's narration goes into another model telling that condenses time:

> After that things seemed to move irreversibly forward. We moved and then moved again. We lived in no one house more than eight months. Rented houses; houses leased with an option to buy; shared houses on the city limits, brick and stucco and a promise to buy; friends of friends who knew somebody had a place standing empty; houses where the owner lived downstairs, next door, next block over, or was a friend of a man had an eye on Mama ... We moved so often Mama learned to keep the newspapers in the cardboard dish barrels and the pads and cords in boxes.
>
> (Allison, Bastard, pp. 64–5)

The model telling is interrupted for an instant, when Annie says, 'Don't throw that away. I'll need that again before long.' Exactly where Annie is physically when she says this is omitted, and then Allison compresses time once again with the following: 'The lines in Mama's face sank deeper with every move, every failed chance, every "make do" and "try again." It got to where I hated moving worse than anything' (Allison, *Bastard*, p. 65).

Throughout this section of the chapter, Allison goes back and forth between model tellings and mini scenes. Her deft handling of forms heightens and dramatises the impact of poverty on Bone without beating you over the head with it for hundreds of pages. Do a close reading of any of your favourite novels, and you will most likely find examples where the author uses similar strategies and others to condense time right in the flow of the prose. After all, not every moment in a novel has enough creative 'soap' and potential imagery to stand as a major scene. Rest assured, however, that Allison has plenty of those too within the pages of *Bastard out of Carolina*.

In *Oxherding tale*, Charles Johnson often uses dates as time-markers. Andrew informs the reader:

> the war between these two families [the Hawkins and the Polkinghorns] focused, as it were, on me, and I found myself caught from my fifth year forward in their crossfire. It started in 1843 when Jonathan realised he would have no children, what with Anna holed up with his flintlock and twenty-five rounds of ammunition in one half of the house.
>
> (Johnson, *Oxherding tale*, p. 8)

In less than two sentences, the story has progressed approximately five years and nine months beyond the wife-swapping incident. And check out this 'bulleted' use of historical facts and dates that Johnson uses while bringing the story to a close:

> On April 23, 1861, Wife bore a girl – six pounds, six ounces – delivered by Dr. Undercliff, who took leave of this life on the event of Grant's capture of Fort Hendry ... Flo Hatfield did not marry again, but took the Vet as her final lover, and in Illinois – in 1865 – Reb built his finest coffin, the one in which they laid Abraham Lincoln to rest. After the war, Fruity and I turned to the business of rebuilding, with our daughter Anna (all is conserved; all), the world.
> This is my tale.
>
> (Johnson, *Oxherding tale*, p. 176)

Lastly, here is an example of Flaubert's timeline management in *Madame Bovary*. What do you notice about it?

> Six weeks passed. Rodolphe [Emma's lover] did not come [to see Emma] again. At last one evening he appeared. The day after the fair he told himself:
> 'Let's not go back too soon; that would be a mistake.'
> And at the end of a week he had gone off hunting. After the hunting he first feared that too much time had passed, and then he reasoned thus:
> 'If she loved me from the first day, impatience must make her love me even more. Let's persist!'
> And he knew that his calculation had been right when, on entering the room, he saw Emma turn pale.
> (Flaubert, *Madame Bovary*, p. 124)

Flaubert often gets accused by twenty-first-century readers of being too wordy with his long descriptive passages, but when he wants to move his story forwards or backwards in time, he often does it in the blink of a phrase.

Among the many lessons you can learn from studying how authors manage the timeline in their prose pieces is that they are constantly doing it to one extent or another, all the while keeping an eye on how best to heighten the story from moment to moment while simultaneously keeping readers informed as to how events fall into place chronologically. Indeed, some stories test a reader's patience in regard to the latter, but there is always a risky point at which a person will grow frustrated with a dizzying, what-happened-when confusion of events and be compelled to put the book, short story or essay down before finishing it. And that is the writer's worst nightmare.

Conclusion

I hope that the suggestions discussed in this chapter on how to read like a writer will serve as directional signs and minimise your chances of getting lost on your journey to becoming an author, and make the artistic road on which you are bravely choosing to travel a lot less riddled with potholes and detours. Crossing the divide between what published writers are able to accomplish on a page and actually doing something similar in your own writing can feel daunting but is by no means impossible. Trust too, that your *voice*, when fully realised, is as one-of-a-kind as your fingerprints. All writers can use some personalised guidance and feedback on their work from mentors and peers alike. In a creative writing programme, your teachers will undoubtedly remind you that writing is a process. The works of prose you read and so greatly admire did not come out of any given author's pen in one fell swoop and were the result of many revisions and drafts. Be dogged in the study and development of your craft, for that, more than any natural talent, is a writer's ticket to success.

Note

1 The Story Workshop® method employs word, oral telling, reading aloud and in-class writing activities to develop writing, reading and problem-solving skills.

Chapter Four

Pre-writing: how to use journals, notes and plans to improve your writing

Lorna Fergusson

What is pre-writing?

Pre-writing refers to a wide range of techniques by which you can approach and get to know your writing project before you 'officially' embark on it. These techniques range all the way from thinking about and discussing a project to mind-mapping, free-writing, journaling, note-taking, planning and research. In this chapter we'll explore how you can employ pre-writing in ways that will increase your confidence in your writing project and enhance your ability to tackle it successfully. This is especially important when you're setting out to write a novel or complete a project of significant length and substance. Used effectively, pre-writing techniques can improve your chances of entering the 'zone' of writing when you commit yourself to producing your story.

Why pre-write?

There are many potential benefits and learning experiences to be had from pre-writing. It allows you to experiment with possibilities without feeling that you've committed yourself too seriously. By testing the potential of ideas you can clarify which ones have the capacity to sustain your creative interest over the long haul.

Through pre-writing, you can practise observation, garner useful material and experiment with expression, structure and point of view. This may save you time later, as you will have had the chance to discover what doesn't work at an early stage rather than when you're halfway through a manuscript and you find out that the structure won't hold up or the perspective you've opted for won't work out. It can help to reduce the chance of experiencing the sort of crisis in confidence that can lead to giving up entirely because it seems easier *not* to write than to get it wrong. If you feel you've had time to play around with your idea and explore its facets, then you may feel greater faith in it and in your ability to tackle it.

At the pre-writing stage, you can also do background research and analysis, which will ground your work and may well lead to new inspirations and connections, lending your story more depth and resonance.

Pre-writing allows you privacy: this is work you don't need to expose to external judgement. Awareness that this is work entirely for *you* can liberate you, not just from the criticism of others but also from your own critical self. At the same time, this playfulness can be combined with discipline, because pre-writing also gives you the chance to get into the mindset of being a committed writer. At the pre-writing stage, you can learn how to create conditions and routines which will be conducive to the regular production of work: this will also contribute to a satisfying degree of momentum when you come to write your project in full.

Pre-writing: tools and techniques

There are various techniques you can employ at the pre-writing stage. In some cases, these involve using physical, tangible resources. At other times, it's about tuning into the intangible, the inspirational – being able to access special states of mind.

THINKING

This seems self-evident, doesn't it? You can't tackle any project unless you think about it. First you have to have your idea or ideas, then you have to think yourself through the maze of plot, the kind of tone and intention you have, the themes you want to explore. So the first thing to take on board is this: to brood is good! You should never underestimate the importance of taking time to think your way into a project. Dennis Palumbo, a psychotherapist who specialises in tackling psychological blocks to creativity, describes in his book *Writing from the inside out* how those around you may see you as a dreamer or daydreamer but that your perspective on yourself should always be that you are a writer-in-training.

What's crucial is that your thinking has a *point*, ultimately. Ideas often cannot be rushed, but they do need to have a purpose. So there's a paradox here. You need a kind of withdrawal into your own private inner space, first of all. You need to take yourself away from distraction. Distraction takes many forms for writers: social life, forms of entertainment, social networking! The world is busy and present to us twenty-four hours a day. It's hard to resist checking our Twitter feeds and our Facebook pages. It's hard to resist going down to the bar. However, it's no accident that, throughout history, people have gone on retreats to get away from the buzz and clutter of society. They've retreated into caves and deserts, they've fasted and performed religious rituals – and have been rewarded by insight into deeper aspects of existence. So it is with writers: I don't mean that you should take up residence in the Kalahari. To retreat is, ultimately, to go within *yourself*. You have to go inside yourself to find out what's there. People choose physical retreat as a means of attaining a psychological or spiritual retreat.

Writing retreats take many forms, from the organised trip to a Greek island or French villa, to a Vermont farmhouse or cottage in Ireland. It can be a weekend away, on your own. It can be a desk at the library, or upstairs in your bedroom. Although we may dream of the perfect retreat, remember that it entails a psychological as much as a physical turning to a place within your head, where you settle into the mindset of the writer. Choose the location that works best for you and indulge yourself in the rituals of the right desk, pen, paper or writing software. Get into the habit of associating that place or those accessories with the process of writing.

A few lines back I mentioned a paradox and it's this: you need to back off from life, yes. You need to go within yourself, yes. You need to accept that to brood is good. But you also need to know when the time for thinking is over and the time for the actual writing has arrived. I'll come back to this point later on, but file it away in the meantime.

COMPOSTING

Composting, to use a gardening image, is about giving a story time to come into being. The word itself, though deeply unglamorous, describes a process, one which can't be rushed, during which ideas settle and bed down within you. Like the slow accumulation of leaf mould, random notions, thoughts, opinions and experiences drift down into the subconscious. They blend and turn into a mulch (another rather unglamorous word) of creative potential from which stories can grow. Allow yourself to be open to notions and experiences but also accept that many writers find a story emerges an exceedingly long time *after* the original experience. In some cases years pass, during which time the notion quietly ferments until it's time for it to fizz its way up to the conscious mind and executive will of the writer.

FREE-WRITING

As all that talk of composting may have made you feel pretty impatient, we'll move on to more 'active' ways of generating story, with more immediate results. You may well have heard of the term 'free-writing' before, or you may have heard of 'morning pages'. These are techniques advocated by such inspirational writers as Dorothea Brande, Julia Cameron and Natalie Goldberg (who also advocates composting). Their aim is to help writers find the sources of inspiration within themselves along with a belief that what the writer does is important and life-affirming. This is a field where writing meets life-coaching, because these are techniques that often have a therapeutic effect on the writer.

So, what does free-writing actually mean? Well, the clue is in the title. The point of the exercise is to liberate your imagination from the constraints of self-consciousness.

41

You take some paper, you may if you choose set a timer, you put pen to paper, and you *write*. You write fast. You write without thinking. You certainly write without editing.

'Morning pages' are precisely that: they're pages you write each morning before the day claims you, with all its distractions, tasks and niggles. When you wake, your mind is often in a strange state, a halfway zone between sleep and full consciousness, and it's in this mental state that imagination can be very active and uninhibited, if you let it – and if you write your thoughts and impressions down before they fade, defeated by the reality of your daily schedule. It's like pinning down dreams: if you don't do it fast then you know you had a dream but you can't for the life of you remember what it was. Seize the moment, seize the feeling, run with it.

To help this process, some people advocate not even lifting the pen from the paper as you write. So, you ask, what *do* I write? You write anything, essentially. Any thought, image, memory, character, description that pops into your mind – and you throw it onto the page any old how. If you come to the end of a phrase or sentence and you can't think what to write next, keep repeating the previous phrase over and over until the log-jam breaks and you can get going again.

Don't think about spelling, grammar or punctuation as you write: this is not the finished article or anything like it, and it's not meant to be. Don't worry if you think you're writing garbage. It doesn't matter. This is all about spontaneity.

One of the purposes here is to create a habit of writing; Julia Cameron in *The artist's way* recommends that you write three pages first thing, every morning. You're making a daily appointment to write. If you discover that mornings are really not your thing, you can turn up in the dead of night, when the world's gone to bed, leaving you able to tap into that strange half-world of nocturnal creativity.

You'll start to build up these free-written pages at a remarkable rate if you maintain your commitment to turning up and writing them. At some point after that initial writing splurge you'll come back to them and review them. As you do, highlight or extract words, images, phrases and notions that jump out at you as interesting. You'll be surprised what's there – at times it will almost feel as if someone else has written the material. In a sense that's true: the someone else was the inner you. Notice what has risen from your subconscious. What themes and feelings turn out to have been significant to you? Do you return to these over and over again? These may have enormous potential as they are so personal. The next stage is to start the process of stepping back from the intimate in order to create the art.

For instance, you may notice the image of a dark room or the word 'abandonment' or the line 'Don't leave me!' crops up. Maybe this has come from personal experience, but now you can start to imagine a character, a *someone else*, who's having this experience. You can alter the context. Maybe as a child your parent forgot one day to pick you up from school: now imagine you're the parent who's forgotten their child. Why would they do that? What are they feeling as they rush towards the school, held up by traffic, consumed by guilt?

Thus, story is born.

Mind-mapping/clustering

If you feel daunted, or all at sea with the idea of free-writing, you might prefer a more visual, organised and constructed method whereby you can allow your mind to come up with connections and directions. Mind-mapping, also known as 'clustering', is a technique you may well have come across before. It allows you to start with a keyword and blitz your way through a set of connected notions that come up, triggered by that central keyword. Mind-mapping gives you a visual sense of your work and the possible directions it may take, which may help you to feel the freedom to play around but at the same time have confidence that your ideas can possess both structure and development.

You can choose to mind-map in an almost doodly manner: just jot down a word. It could be a theme at the heart of what you want to write. 'War', say, or 'doomed love' or 'betrayal'. Then start to jot down connected ideas, linking them back to the central one. You might play around with 'betrayal', taking it off in the direction of betrayal in 'business' or 'sport' or 'society', by 'a friend' or 'a lover'. Mind-mapping essentially creates a halo of possibilities, each of which generates its own halo.

You can use computer software such as Mindjet to help the process of mind-mapping: the end result is a visual map of potentiality. Just don't doodle and play for too long!

Talking (and listening)

Like thinking, this seems to be all too obvious to be called a technique. However, many writers shy away from discussing their work with others. They're inhibited by the fear that the inner critic they live with will be reinforced by the outer critic, whose comments will devalue their work, highlight its failings – and, by extension, the writer's failings as a human being. To talk about your work takes courage. In some cases, it takes ego: the mirror of the shy retiring writer is the arrogant writer who takes centre-stage and does nothing *but* talk.

Who should you be talking to? There are all sorts of possibilities. Of course there are your friends and family, your nearest and dearest. The risk here is that they care too much about you to give you honest feedback or that they think, fondly, that putting you down will keep that writer-ego in check. It might be better to consider talking to fellow writers, who will understand all too well the struggles you're having. Or mentors and writing tutors, people who not only have experience of the process of writing but who are able to suggest practical strategies for solving problems.

You should also be *listening*, of course. As a writer, you should have your radar switched on all the time for what could make a story. Be shameless about this. Listen to conversations and write them down. You are always listening for the potential in people's experiences and attitudes. If you're a fiction-writer, remember you're at liberty to bend reality. You can add new characters, change dates and places, alter the sequence and pace of events. Use reality as a springboard into your imagined world.

JOURNALING

This, arguably, is the most obvious technique of all. It's well known that many writers' first novels tend to be autobiographical, and certainly your own life can provide more material than you ever thought possible.

The best way to develop your writing skills in combination with what you can source from your life is to start journaling or diary writing. As with free-writing, you are liberated by the idea, first of all, that you are writing a private document. Diaries and journals require you to be honest. You aim for authenticity in the way you describe events and your personal reactions to those events. You aim for honesty in the expression of those events, which is an excellent way of improving your powers of observation and analysis. You train your writer's eye and ear: knowing you will later describe what has happened, in the pages of your diary or journal, works wonders to sharpen your awareness.

A diary asks of you that you record each day in it. For some people that works very well indeed. It provides a discipline in that you know you should be writing in it every month, every week, every year. It provides a linear shape. On New Year's Eve you can cast your eye back over the significant moments of your year and feel glad that you captured both the dramatic and the more mundane events.

For others, a diary is a tyranny. Those dates at the top of the page nag and chivvy. If a day is missed the writer feels guilty, intends to go back and fill in the blanks, perhaps never does – perhaps lets the whole thing lapse. Guilt and resentment are not good for creativity.

A journal, then, may be the answer: here you choose on which days you will open those pages and write. If you have nothing to say, you say nothing. If you're brimming with words, they can flow on for page after page because you're not trammelled by the limits of your diary's allocated page or half page. This gives you freedom to spread your wings but doesn't send you on a guilt trip if your wings are clipped.

In your journal you can write about emotions without them being linked to a specific day's events. You can write responses to films or shows, you can write a debate about an issue that concerns you, you can write a manifesto for yourself as an artist, you can create a 'commonplace book' effect by recording wise words and favourite lines and what they mean to you. You can use your journal as your ideas book, you can record what you're currently working on and how you feel about it at each stage, what lessons you've learned, what plans you've made.

Life-mining is also about the experiences of others: it isn't always all about you. If you want to enrich your perceptions of human nature, record lives other than your own. Read memoirs and biographies, newspaper articles, interviews, history and social history, look at old photographs. View all of these as potential sources for plots and characters. The old adage that truth is stranger than fiction? True.

NOTING

Ideas can come ... they can also go. All too often you think you'll retain an inspired or salient thought, but then it slips from your grasp. Our headspaces are crowded, and we are easily distracted, so you need to write down more than your personal history and core emotions in diaries and journals. You need to record information, research, plot notes, possible character names, possible titles for stories (always a fun activity). If you overhear an amazing conversation on a bus, you need to keep it recorded and fresh.

The prime rule of the game is always *always* to have a notebook by you. As an alternative, you might like to use a digital recorder as an aural 'jotter' – though don't use it to record overheard conversations! Keep a notebook by the bed. This is crucial because of that strange brain-state I mentioned earlier, when you are between sleep and waking, a state that allows ideas to rise to the surface, along with beautiful phrases and sudden perceptions. There isn't a writer alive who hasn't sleepily said to himself or herself, 'Oh, I'll remember that in the morning' only to find that in the cold light of day the Muse is long gone. It's incredibly frustrating to know that for the lack of a little bit of effort you've let something go which could have been great. So, keep that notebook by the bed. And a pen that works.

Many writers – and you may be one – are complete notebookaholics. They cannot come out of a stationer's shop without having bought a notebook. They're engaged in a quest for the Holy Grail of notebooks, with perfect paper, margin size, smoothness, portability ... The problem with notebookaholics is that they accumulate virgin notebooks they cannot bring themselves to taint with actual writing, because writing runs the risk of being imperfect. So they save their notebooks, waiting for the perfect expression of the perfect project. You have to accept that perfection never comes.

Many writers write on whatever old scrap of paper comes to hand. This is because inspiration isn't very considerate, tending to arrive at the most inopportune moments. So you end up with torn off pieces of paper, envelopes, bus tickets, with something scrawled on them – something which later is indecipherable or cryptic to you. Jotting down notes randomly is good in that you've captured that moment's thought, but you should take the process further. You can transfer notes into notebooks or onto the computer. You can use a programme like Evernote, for example, which sits on your toolbar and which can be brought up in an instant. You can create a new category, a 'note' on it and record your thought or phrase: it's safe. You can sync Evernote with your mobile devices so that if you're out and about, once again, the moment's thought is captured.

You can also use writing software such as Scrivener, which gives you not only increased flexibility when creating and moving around sections of your story but has an onscreen area where you can save research notes, links and images.

Some writers like to use wall charts and pinboards where they attach photos, maps and timelines as a way of containing information. You could pin up photos of actors who resemble your imagined characters, or pictures of costumes, or maps of battlefields or shipping routes – whatever is relevant to the story you envisage.

Planning

From notes, you move to more ordered plans. This is where you start to draw connections and approach your work in terms of its sequence and how it will all hang together. By this stage, you're no longer feeling about in the dark. You've explored potential notions and have found that some simply don't have the 'legs' to be taken further. A good story always flags up how good it is by the way it grows in your mind. As in the mind-map we discussed earlier, your central idea will have sprouted feelers and may have shot off in lots of different directions. But now, as you prepare to engage with serious composition, it may need pruning and taming. You could draw your plot as a graph or set out its stages in a series of index cards which you can move around. Draw sketches and timelines, set out the line of your plot, with its crises and turning points. Give yourself a map. Try to get a sense of the 'arc', the potential trajectory of your story. To enrich characterisation, you can 'hot-seat' your invented characters, quizzing them about their backgrounds and beliefs, building up a solid sense of who they are. Many details about them may not make it into the finished story, but by exploring aspects of their biographies you give yourself and your reader a greater sense that they have an existence 'off the page'. If you start believing in your characters to the point where you instinctively know what they would or would not do in a given situation, then your reader is likely to believe in them too.

Research

You can also research background fact and detail for your story. You may need to know the kind of terrain on which a battle was fought, so you use Google satellite as well as historians' accounts. You may need to know about women's fashions in the 1940s so you need to read women's magazines of the era or watch movies. You may need to know how it felt to wear a suit of armour in the fourteenth century, so find out whether there's a medieval re-enactment society whose members can tell you. If you're writing non-fiction, clearly you need to prioritise accuracy and you need to be prepared to put hours into fact-checking. If you're writing fiction, the act of gathering information often has an inspirational effect, throwing up connections or surprising elements you couldn't have imagined on your own. You may need to spend time in libraries and archives, you may use the Internet (judiciously), you may want to travel to particular locations or interview useful witnesses or people with experience of the subject of your story.

READING

Some writers are wary of reading other writers' works for fear of being influenced, but it's important that you read widely and often. Developing the skill of critical reading can help you to understand what works and what does not work. You can then bring this skill to bear on your own work both while you create it and later, when you revise it. You should try to cultivate a dispassionate critical awareness of your own writing abilities and strive continually to improve.

PLAYING

At the pre-writing stage you can experiment with subjects and with writing styles. By telling yourself that you're not as yet actually committed to either subject or approach, that you're just taking your lines for a walk, you can feel unburdened, unpressured. Much of the emphasis of these pre-writing strategies has been on their spontaneous and liberated qualities, because once a writer feels forced to write in a certain way, they can become inhibited, and inhibition and self-criticism can lead to the dreaded writer's block. So tell yourself continually that nothing you have written is set in stone and that if one approach does not play out well, you can experiment with another.

Timetabling

Although I've just mentioned playful experimentation, it is also worthwhile making a deal with yourself to work regularly and committedly. Thus, experiment takes place within the structure of a disciplined and mature approach to writing. In the free-writing section earlier I discussed making an appointment with yourself: decide when you work best as a writer, whether it's early in the morning, late at night, at weekends. Challenge yourself to turn up, again and again, even when the spirit isn't really moving you, and write. Experiment with a timetable chart for the composition of your project, especially if it's a long one, working out set dates by which you will complete the first 5,000 or 10,000 words, or dividing the work into quarters with date targets and setting a completion date for the entire project.

Buddying

Many writers find it useful to set up a buddying relationship with another writer. This can boost both morale and productivity because here you make a deal with somebody else that you will turn up and write, that you will produce certain amounts by certain dates. Each buddy supports and is answerable to the other. You agree to deliver segments of work at set times: you meet up and discuss what you're doing. You are prepared to be a comfort, a support and at times an outright nag – and you expect your buddy to be the same.

The downside of pre-writing

Writers are very talented when it comes to the art of displacement activity, so be careful! Preparing to write can all too easily take the place of actual writing. You can toy with too many ideas and projects or tell yourself that you need to do just a little bit more research and then you'll be ready ... You may have talked about it so much that even you are bored with it. You find yourself working in fitful bursts but you achieve no steady momentum. The work stalls. Ultimately, you need to achieve a balance between preparatory work and getting on with the main project, because if you don't you risk losing faith in it and in yourself.

How to avoid the downside?

As I've said before, being answerable really helps here. Be answerable to yourself by setting targets. Create deadlines you must work towards, set goals in terms of word counts and datelines. Just make sure that your goals are realistic and that you are not likely to fall short of them if you make a reasonable effort.

Set up meetings with your writing buddy or mentor. Embarrass yourself into productivity by telling your friends and the entire Twitterverse that you'll enter a certain competition or finish your story by a certain date. Stephen King in *On writing* describes the Muse as a guy who lives in the basement: go down there and hit him on the head until he mends the boiler.

As a prompt, you can write an 'elevator pitch' summing up your story's purpose in a sentence or two. Then pin it up where you can see it, a constant reminder of what is core to your writing project.

Be prepared to go public: your ultimate aim is for people to read your writing, so after the pre-writing and the writing, there's the reception and the reaction to your work. You are moving from the silent room, the room of meditation and experimentation, into the auditorium, where your readers await you.

Don't skip about the surface of things. There comes a time when you need to say, 'This is the project I choose' and make a commitment to it, whether it's a short story or a full novel. Be answerable to the story you feel deserves to be told in the way only you can tell it. Trust your instinct and believe in that story's right to be told and in your voice's right to be heard. Nobody can write this story the way you can. Nobody.

So go write it.

Chapter Five

Workshops: what they are (and aren't) and how to make the most of them

Jennifer Young

Most writers have someone, usually family or friends, who will tell them their writing is superb. However, as fantastic as it feels to hear that your work is excellent, it will not help you to improve as a writer. To do this, you need honest, thoughtful feedback on your writing, and the creative writing workshop is an ideal environment for this to occur. The format, the style and the shape may change depending on your lecturer's style, but the core idea remains the same.

The roots of creative writing in academia can be traced back to 1880 at Harvard University, and the University of Iowa began to accept creative work for degrees in 1922. Throughout the twentieth century, many universities established creative writing programmes, and, along the way, the workshop became the default form of teaching. In the twenty-first century, the basic workshop form is common throughout the world – mainly because it's been proven to work. Many celebrated writers, including Raymond Carver, Joyce Carol Oates, Ian McEwan, Kazuo Ishiguro, Tracy Chevalier and Rita Dove, attended creative writing programmes and workshops. Critics sometimes malign it, but the workshop remains in place primarily because it is successful.

One criticism sometimes levelled at workshops is that participants may not be very experienced writers. They may have published little, if anything at all, by the time they come to attend their first workshop. However, writers or not, we are all bombarded constantly with narrative and imagery through novels, stories, journalism, films, plays, television, poetry and advertising. This experience in reading narratives and imagery will give you the basic skills to enable you to participate in an introductory workshop, and, as you progress through your studies, you will become increasingly proficient readers and editors of creative work. As your skills in reading others' writing develops, your ability to edit and read your own will also increase. Furthermore, the skills you from workshopping (such as editing, giving and receiving feedback and working effectively in small groups) will stay with you long after you've completed your creative writing course, whether you become a published writer or not.

This chapter will explore the structure of a workshop and then consider best practice within the workshop, both when your own work is being discussed and when you contribute as a reader and editor.

The structure of a workshop

A workshop is, in its most basic sense, a space where writing is discussed. It gives you a rare chance to get a group of people to pay very close attention to your work. In most undergraduate workshops, you will read some published work, complete some writing exercises (in and out of class) and workshop your own and other students' writing. Reading is discussed in more detail elsewhere in this book, but remember as you workshop that the reading you are assigned (and the reading you complete generally in your life) will influence the way you discuss writing. As you read, think about the techniques and the craft decisions the authors have made. These are the same craft and technique choices that face you as you write, and discussion of these choices in relation to the writing you have produced will benefit both your own writing and that of your peers.

Workshops give you an excellent opportunity to improve your writing. They aren't a place for therapy, airing your political views, carrying out personal vendettas or imposing your will on everyone else. Nor can any workshop promise to make you a best-selling author. But workshops can help you to improve what you write. Workshops also are not a place for you to submit a half-done piece of writing and wait for a committee to finish it for you. You will garner ideas, suggestions and feedback, but it will not magically improve a piece of writing you have not put time and energy into creating. While workshopping may improve your grade, in that you have gained readers who will copy-edit, that should not be your only motivation for workshopping.

When you enter into a workshop, you are entering into a collegiate relationship with your fellow participants, whether you are a BA student, a postgraduate or a published writer. Think of the workshop, no matter how informal, as part of your professional activity as a writer. The other participants are your fellow writers, your associates and not simply 'students'. In other subjects you might take, the student sitting next to you will be discussing subjects such as literature, history, archaeology, chemistry, etc.

The discussion is generally prompted or led by the teacher, and the content you are studying has been created or discovered by a person who is either long dead or at least living and working somewhere else.

In contrast, in a creative writing workshop, you and the people sitting around you have created the content. You are engaging in professional activity by creating, presenting and discussing writing. The professional nature of the classroom should engender an ethos of supportive, encouraging yet honest feedback and respect for your fellow writers. Approaching all the participants as professional colleagues also means that your behaviour within the workshop needs to be of a certain standard. This certainly doesn't mean that you have to dress as if for an interview or never laugh at jokes. The best part of being in a workshop is the strong relationships that build up between participants, particularly if you remain the same group for a period of time. You will probably know the students in your creative writing workshop better than those in any other class. Yet with established, clear boundaries, you can personally make a workshop more productive and enjoyable for everyone.

When you first begin workshopping, the lecturer or leader is likely to be quite active. She or he will guide the group and may prompt people to expand on their comments. She or he may also offer their own suggestions. As you advance through your career as a writer, student writers will begin to play a much larger role in the workshop. This increased responsibility will be discussed later in the chapter.

When fellow students give you their work to read, you are being asked to do a great favour. You also have a fantastic opportunity to have other people read your work. But how do you participate in the workshop to gain the maximum benefit, both for yourself and your fellow writers?

Your own work

The workshopping method can improve your writing because you gain new readers. Your workshop colleagues are far better able to gain an overview of your piece than you are: they come to it cold, just as a reader picking up a book in a shop does. They can ask questions that might seem obvious to you (of course the background of character X includes Y!), but their questions can raise issues that you have not noticed. Considering answers to these questions may also resolve or solidify ideas or concepts you had been pondering but had not yet made a firm decision on.

If your work is scheduled for discussion, share it in a timely manner. Remember that people have busy lives, so it might not be convenient to read it at the last minute. Make your copy as 'clean' as possible; edit it several times. While it is useful to get copy-editing feedback, it's usually more useful to get substantive feedback, not extensive notes on spelling and grammar. Speak calmly about your work. Try your best to avoid being defensive: remember that the feedback you receive in a workshop is far more considerate than anything you're likely to get back after you've finished your education and are sending out manuscripts 'for real'.

Sometimes it can be difficult to put your work forward. Maybe life interfered, and you only had an hour to work on it rather than two, or maybe you just couldn't manage to get the piece to come out properly. Perhaps you have spent hours and hours on your work, but the thought of giving it to other people to read makes you feel just a little bit sick. All of this is perfectly normal. However, no matter how nervous you feel, try your absolute best to avoid saying, 'Here's my story/poem/play/scene, but it's really rubbish.' A negative approach puts undue pressure on your fellow writers. They will either (1) see it only as a poor piece of work and seek out the flaws you have so clearly declared to exist, or (2) be as nice as possible about the piece to try to build up your confidence. The latter is far more likely to occur in a workshop environment, especially if a group is new to workshopping. Neither is particularly useful to you, and it makes your colleagues as nervous and distressed as you are.

Workshops usually are structured in one of two ways. In the first, the author cannot speak until the end of the workshop. This means you can't answer questions or defend your decisions. The second method allows for writers to enter into the discussion and answer direct questions. There are advantages to each. The first means that you have to listen more closely. It also means that you do not spend the majority of your workshop talking, which limits how much feedback you can receive. However, being able to speak can help point the workshoppers towards areas you want to discuss: for instance, you can settle at the beginning that something isn't a typo, you did intend for the female character to have green hair, etc.

Most workshops will include a point where you can ask any questions you want to be addressed. Take advantage of this opportunity and prepare some in advance. These can be technical questions (point of view, verb tense, etc.)

or they can be overarching questions about imagery, character, structure or endings. Write them down before you come to the workshop, as it's very easy to forget them once in the workshopping environment. You will not be able to remember everything that is said, so it's also useful to take notes during the workshop. People will often say things aloud they will not write down. Keep notes, or ask a friend to take notes. When the active discussion ends, be polite and thank people for their feedback.

After your workshop ends, allow some time to settle yourself emotionally. It is rare to gain such an intense burst of attention for something you have done. If the discussion has been intense, allow some time to re-establish the dynamic between yourself and the other group members. This is another excellent reason to take notes – you have recorded everything, so you don't need to analyse all your feedback at once. As the group moves on to the next piece to workshop, make sure you participate fully in the next discussion. You can analyse your own workshop after the class ends.

Give yourself some time to reflect on your feedback. Examine the notes from other writers and your lecturer, and look at the notes you have taken in the workshop. You are likely to disagree with at least some of the comments you have received. Sometimes you will receive feedback that bothers you personally. You have spent a huge amount of time crafting your work, and how dare those other writers not recognise the brilliance of it? Dealing with this is an important part of workshopping. Remember that you do not write by a committee. The piece remains yours, and your name alone will appear on it. Do not feel that you have to change your piece to please everyone. There are a few exceptions – *do* correct spelling mistakes, and think seriously about grammar or punctuation feedback you receive. The copy-editing feedback you receive can be very useful, as it can be all too easy to overlook small mistakes.

Think carefully about how you respond to feedback, and remember that your fellow writers are trying to help you. Don't complain loudly about someone who doesn't understand as you leave the room. It's also not a space for a personal vendetta. As you workshop, it is likely you will identify two or three people whose feedback you value highly. It may be that you feel they 'get' your writing, or it may be that they are exceptionally good editors. This is normal and useful. However, do not discount the other voices in the room. Your readership, once you get published, will not only be people who 'get' your work. Reviewers will not always 'get' your work.

Workshopping in an age of social media also brings its own set of challenges. While in the past university workshops used to involve lecturers or students spending time and money photocopying writing and distributing it to the rest of the group, now work is often shared on universities' virtual learning environments (VLEs). Classroom discussions can sometimes extend beyond the official environment into social media such as Facebook or Twitter. Remember to consider this space public (unless your privacy settings are very strict) if you are discussing other participants or their work, and don't post anything online you wouldn't say in front of the group. Other opportunities exist to share your work beyond the classroom, including new online 'writers' workshops' and other reading groups. Some of these are run by reputable organisations, such as publishers or agents, but others are not. Always investigate these carefully before you post your work, and certainly before you pay anyone to edit your work.

The work of others

Creative writing workshops generally focus on the writing of a few participants per session, which allows for each piece of work to undergo substantive discussion. Your work will probably not be discussed every week, but think about how you want to be treated in a workshop and extend the same courtesy to other people in the group when it's their turn to have their work discussed. Make sure that you attend each session if you are at all capable of making it. Pay attention – which means don't whisper to the people sitting around you, don't text or surf the web and definitely don't fall asleep!

Even if you feel anxious about contributing to the workshop, it is still important to attend. There will always be a few members of every workshop group who seem to have a lot to say about every single piece, and that can feel intimidating if you are a quieter person. However, the one short, pertinent comment you have to offer may be more useful to the author than all the rest. Moreover, you are constantly learning in a workshop. If writer A has an issue with characterisation, the suggestion writer B gives might just help with your own writing. As has been mentioned before, learning to be a better editor of others' work can be extremely useful in translating back to editing your own work.

In a writing workshop, you may be asked to read work that is completely different to what you would read for pleasure. You might be reading horror, sci-fi, literary fiction, etc. Whatever the genre, always remember you are reading with an eye to improving the writing.

Often, workshops are arranged in a circle or square, so you can see everyone. Even though the lecturer is leading or moderating the workshop, do not address all of your comments to him or her. Address your comments to the person whose work you are discussing. The lecturer does not need to know that changing a word on page three will improve the piece – the author does. Making eye contact while giving feedback is an excellent way to maintain the respect levels and friendliness in a workshop. Sometimes lecturers will want you to jump into the workshop when you have something to add. Some lecturers will go around the room, asking each student to alternate with praise and something constructive. Each workshop leader will have their own style, so this chapter will address best practice for giving feedback generally.

As a first step, prepare for the workshop and be ready to address the work under consideration. If you have been asked to read a piece in advance, read it in advance. If at all possible, try to read through each piece twice. For the first time, read it as you normally would for enjoyment. See where the piece goes, think about the plot, the narrative or the structure of the poem. Look at it in a macro level. If you bought this in a bookshop, what would you think? The second time through, read it on a micro level. Think about the function of each word, each image, each line. Read some of the dialogue aloud. Throughout this process, keep notes. If these notes are for you alone, you can be as blunt as you like. Write down everything you think about the piece. Given the pressures of university life, it's likely you'll often walk into the workshop room having come from other classes, and you may have read the work late the night before, or even a day or two ago. It can be very easy to forget your reactions, and no author wants to hear that you had a very good idea but you forgot it on the bus. Make notes about each piece – ideally on a printed copy of the text, or on a bit of paper you can then give to the author.

Authors may have a chance to raise issues in advance of the workshop, for example, saying they are unsure if the ending works and they would welcome ideas. 'Ideas' mean just that – they aren't asking you to write the ending for them. Comments from the group may trigger a new spark of inspiration for them, but they are under no obligation to apply all the suggestions in the notes. As mentioned before, no one writes by committee, so don't be offended if authors don't implement your brilliant idea for them.

Try to consider the author's requests, but also formulate your own questions and suggestions. This does not mean suggesting that a story they've set in New York in the 1980s should be set in space because you like science fiction. Nor does it mean that you need to make suggestions about how to make it more like your own writing. You might instead comment that the fashion of the 1980s doesn't appear much in the work, and you think mentioning clothing could really enhance the setting or the development of character X. Similarly, if you are reading work that uses very concrete metaphors and you prefer abstract metaphors, do not tell the other writer they are doing it incorrectly. Instead, consider how the imagery works throughout the poem. If, for example, in the middle of a

65

series of nature images, an image of urban decay pops up, think about whether the transition works or if it jars.

Once you enter a workshop, certain types of feedback are best avoided. The worst possible thing to say in a workshop is 'I really liked it' and stop. While it is lovely to hear, it does absolutely nothing for the writer in terms of improving their work. Immediately follow up with a comment that specifies why you thought it was good, such as 'I liked the portrayal of the character', 'I liked the use of rhythm'. Be specific. 'The use of rhythm in the second stanza is very strong, particularly in line three.' This also allows you to follow up with what could be improved. 'The image in the fourth line isn't as concrete as it is in line six', or 'the character does something on page three that seems completely out of character based on what happens on the previous two pages.'

Only through specifics can the author see how a piece may be improved. Think both small-scale and large-scale. Examine the work sentence by sentence and any poetry line by line. Think about the choices behind each word. At the same time, think about larger questions, such as the overarching tone of the piece, the creation of characters, the voice, the point at which the piece begins and ends. Does the title fit? Is there a title?

Avoid attacking the writer personally. Always assume that the narrator is not the author (unless you are in a life-writing or creative-non-fiction class). Avoid saying, 'the way you killed the mother on page three': make it clear that you are discussing the character's actions. The character's actions are not the same as the author's! Remember when you are talking about the work that the person who wrote it is in the room, not dead or in another country or city like in a literature or history class. Even if your best friend in the world is in the group, do not tease them about the writing *or* give their work lavish and unwarranted praise. Treat their work exactly the same – as a professional colleague.

As mentioned before, early on in a workshop, your lecturer will prompt you to go further in your feedback. Try to avoid single statements – even positive ones such as 'It's perfect, I can't find anything to fault.' Again, a comment like this is lovely to hear, but not very helpful. In a workshop, you are not necessarily looking for 'faults'. You want to stretch a piece further, pushing both the work and the writer to take it to a higher level of creativity, expertise and fluency.

Raymond Carver wrote that 'Evan Connell said once that he knew he was finished with a short story when he found himself going through and taking out commas and then going through the same story and putting commas back in the same places … I respect that kind of care for what is being done' (Carver, 'On writing', p. 24). You want to take similar care both with your own writing and with that of your fellow writers in your workshop. You should also apply Carver's advice to your own writing – and learn to know when you need to stop editing!

Getting the balance right in feedback

This chapter has discussed the two extremes of workshop feedback, from what we might call the 'I really liked it' approach to the personal attack. Where does the balance lie between constructive criticism and destructive criticism? In part, that balance is achieved in tone of your feedback. For example, when I was an undergraduate, a student in my workshop put forward a story. The main character was brilliantly written as a truly terrible character who hurt everyone around her. I said, 'I really hate this character because' but the other writer clearly never heard my 'because'. He went bright red and stayed upset with me for some time. It is vitally important to be honest in your feedback, but it is worth pausing for half a second to consider how to phrase your feedback. The tone you strike is particularly important.

As your creative writing expertise increases, your lecturer will probably start to take a diminished role in the workshop. As you and your colleagues contribute more to the workshop, finding that balanced line is increasingly important. The best policy is to give very detailed feedback. For basic-level editing – spelling, vocabulary, syntax – make a note of it on the copy of the student's work or on a spare sheet of paper and hand it to them. This frees up time to have substantive conversation about a piece – what Spencer Jordan's chapter on editing calls 'summative editing', the bigger picture. Rely on the notes you made while reading the piece. If the piece is presented in class, take notes as it is being read. You may find that you disagree with something another writer in the group says about the piece under discussion. Say so. It can be very useful to a writer to have two colleagues discuss their views about a particular issue. A forthright debate between two or more members of the workshop will be beneficial for the writer to hear. It reminds everyone that viewpoints differ, and, between themselves, the two workshoppers may come to agree with a different view. Furthermore, in discussing another student's work, you may also want to argue passionately for some point, and you should. Just make certain you maintain that same level of respect.

You will find that you will not please everyone when you come to submit your work to agents or editors. When you send your work out, remember the differing viewpoints you have heard in your workshop and remember that agents and publishers similarly have conflicting opinions. For instance, both William Golding's *Lord of the flies* and J. K. Rowling's *Harry Potter and the philosopher's stone* received multiple rejections before eventually being published with great success.

Workshops are also invaluable for teaching you how to let go of your pieces. Regular workshopping can not only improve your writing, it can also improve your confidence, which means you are able to submit your work more easily.

Workshopping after university

Students on most creative writing programmes churn out writing at a pace that can be difficult to maintain after formal education. This speed of creation means that writing is often workshopped quite quickly. Having immediate feedback on work can be both an advantage and a disadvantage. Enthusiasm from your workshop can spur you on to finish the work, or a lukewarm response can make you want to drop it completely. Consider when is best for you put forward a piece. Keep in mind that you are showing a work in progress, so don't let the reaction of your workshop turn you completely off something.

After you leave formal education, if you decide to pursue a career as a writer, you will receive feedback from professionals. Your aim will be to get your writing in front of agents, editors and publishers, and you will long to receive feedback from them. However, as noted above, the feedback they send is likely to be far more brutal than anything you receive in a workshop. Many writers continue in workshops they organise themselves after leaving university in order to continue to receive feedback. Think about asking the people from your university workshop who you got along with particularly well to stay in touch and keep discussing writing.

Conclusion

Workshops allow you to connect with others and gain vital feedback to improve your work. They won't make your creations perfect or guarantee financial success, but the supportive and challenging environment they provide can be just the spur you need to get your work to a publishable standard. Two key points to remember: you don't write by a committee. It will be your name on the final product, so make sure you are happy with it. And second, your workshop participants want to help you: they are generously sharing their time and attention. Treat them as you want to be treated, and respect their writing just as they respect yours.

Chapter Six

Online learning and how it can help your work

Elizabeth Reeder

Introduction

Increasingly, almost any learning activity we undertake has an online component. Creative writing is no different, and learning online and learning creative writing are, in many ways, a perfect match. In this chapter I will detail the elements of online learning you're likely to encounter in your writing courses and will also address questions about how online elements can augment learning in a traditional face-to-face classroom. I'll suggest the ways you can make the best use of what online environments have to offer, and the chapter as a whole will help illuminate the ways that learning creative writing online can make you a better writer.

The chapter will also discuss the care and attention we need to use when communicating with people online in forums, workshops and via our written feedback. It will include a discussion of the role of praise, questioning, assessing our own opinions, as well as outline students' responsibilities for building strong discussions within a creative writing course. All writing is practice, and everything you do on an online creative writing course is about becoming a better reader and a better writer.

Pros and cons of learning creative writing online

Learning online can be done from anywhere there's an internet connection, fits around your own schedule and requires personal commitment and responsibility from each student. Additionally, when you're learning writing online, the bulk of your communication is written, and therefore everything you do – in forums and chats and when you give feedback to your peers and read the feedback that has been given to you – is about gaining good critical reading and observation skills. So, all the writing you do while online (and when off) is practising the writing skills you've come to learn.

However, there can be downsides too. Learning in a virtual environment can feel less immediate because it can lack the buzz of a face-to-face class, and this can, in turn, lead to a sense of isolation or distance. Some people can find reading on a screen difficult, and this can be off-putting – although screens are getting more readable and mobile all the time. Online we don't get the same sense of performance as we do in a face-to-face class; you can't read body language, facial expressions or tone of voice, all of which add a lot of humour, subtlety, as well as a necessary awareness about how a group is faring in a classroom. All these facts can make virtual learning feel less involved, and some people find online spaces too virtual and won't be able to engage. Also, some people don't want to spend a lot of time in forums or in a group, and, for them, mentoring or a face-to-face class might be better. The energy of a live class can happen online, but building a sense of community online does take a bit more effort. If everyone commits the time to the course and pays attention to their peers and tutor, we can draw out the strengths of the ways we do communicate. In this situation, the dynamic, word-based nature of the virtual learning environment (VLE), the independent space for thought and consideration, is also one of incredible possibilities.

Learning online is also more 'reading heavy' in that you need to keep up to date by reading all forum posts and live chats (and/or logs), as well as being active online (i.e. writing responses to what you read). This can be great training for writing-related tasks or jobs such as editing or proofreading, but it's also time consuming. If you're participating well you'll be asking questions (and you do need to ask questions, if you have them, because online you're invisible to both the tutor and peers, especially since they can't see your puzzled expression like they can in a class).

You should also be reading the supplementary and essential material and links, which may include links to audio-video or cross-media resources. It's easy to get lost or to fall behind online, and the responsibility for keeping on top of work really does rest with you.

The virtual learning environment (VLE)

There are some radically structured and located courses available online. For instance, some courses take place on Second Life, which is a completely virtual world with avatars, and here classes can take place anywhere imaginable such as in the middle of a forest or the top of a skyscraper. However, most online classes take place in Moodle or WebCT, which are both more straightforward VLEs.

In the virtual classroom, all the information, resources and communication tools of a course are held in a single

73

space, and most learning takes place both 'asynch' (not in 'real' time) via forums, links to podcasts or recordings and other resources. Additionally, some courses include 'live' sessions via webchats or webinars. These live resources often have 'logs' that can be accessed after the live session has ended. Most communications on a VLE or online classroom are held in that virtual space and can be seen by all staff and students, at any time, which makes for easy access and reference.

Online facilities, such as forums or the uploading of resources and links, are often used in campus-based or face-to-face classes in order to streamline submission procedures for workshops or assignments, to increase the availability of resources, and to add to the breadth of communications that can happen among students and between students and tutors.

A good VLE should be relatively easy to understand. Even so, it will still take time to become familiar with. Figure out the ways you work best online. Keep active on the course, ask questions, be aware of the tone and the clarity of everything you write on the course and in all your messages and posting be yourself and be present.

Getting orientated: making your own map

One myth that should be debunked is that online learning takes less time. In my experience it actually takes *more* time – although you do have more control over how and when you learn. Since most resources are held in a written form in any online classroom (in forums, via links, and as downloads), in order to keep up-to-date, you need to take the time to read everything (and it often takes longer to read, than to participate in a discussion) and follow links and also process and respond to the information you're taking in.

It's crucially important to really understand the online environment. As noted above, you'll need to take time at the start of the semester to become familiar with the layout of the course. Spend time at the start of term getting used to how the VLE classroom is laid out and how to navigate between different tools and resources. Taking the time at the start of class to become familiar and comfortable in this online environment will save you time and frustration later on. When you're starting out, I'd encourage you to take notes in a good old-fashioned paper notebook and keep it handy for reference. No one can do this orientating for you. Even the best, most exciting and clearly organised sites still take time to get used to. To think that you don't have to put in this time is like arriving in a new city, without a map, and thinking you'll know where everything is.

Ask questions

Spend time on your own, using resources the tutor provides, but if you get stuck or need a bit of guidance don't hesitate to ask questions. Chances are that if you have questions, other people will be having them too. If you post a question in a forum (see below) the whole class can see it. In this way you're also asking your peers for help or guidance and it's one of the ways to build a sense of community online. When you ask questions (in particular about any IT or navigational aspects of the course), be as specific as possible about what is going on, about what you see, and any other useful information you can provide. If you were in a classroom with loads of computers, the teacher could simply look over your shoulder to see what you see and they'd have the information they need. Online, you need to communicate that information to them so they can best help you problem-solve the issue.

It can be easier to get frustrated or fall behind in an online class and asking questions keeps you orientated and included in the course.

Some tools and resources

All online writing classes will be unique in structure and content and tutors will choose different tools and resources and use them in their own ways. The key here is to familiarise yourself with the course you're on and to ask questions. Put in the time and the start and making best use of the site will be second nature for the rest of the course. Here are a few tools and resources that are found on VLEs and how they're used in creative writing courses.

DISCUSSION FORUMS

A forum is an 'asynch' (not real time) discussion space where you can post and respond to messages. These forums are usually organised by week or subject, and you can either start your own 'thread' or reply to one that's already underway. (Most email systems work according to the same principle, and so the threaded nature of the discussions should be somewhat familiar.) For writing classes forums are ideal for uploading/downloading workshop submissions (and for uploading feedback on the work). All forum discussions and posts are held on the VLE and can be accessed and revisited for reference. Many VLEs also send emails of any forum posts, so they come into your inbox AND you can see them in context, in the forum on the VLE. This can be useful if an email goes astray, or if you simply want to check you've read everything, simply go to the forum and go through the posts.

To make the most of learning online, you need to pay attention to the effectiveness, clarity and tone of all your messages, responses, posts and feedback in all the tools and resources online. Forums are at the very centre of this good writing and communication practice.

LIVE CHATS

Live chats are live discussions that are scheduled like face-to-face classes. In most VLEs, at the moment, these are still text-based. But they are quickly becoming video and audio based (see webinars, below). Although text-based chats can be slower and there's arguably a bit less learning to be had (because fewer topics can be covered in the same amount of time), they do have the great benefit of being 'logged' and you can go back and read a live chat, understand the discussion, or it acts as a record you can access if you missed the discussion. Many people prefer this for workshops or one-to-one tutorials because they can go back and re-read what's said (sometimes when we're being given feedback we can stop listening or seeing everything). Even though I offer telephone tutorials, many people prefer text-based tutorials because they can go back to them and see what's been said verbatim, in context.

ASSIGNMENT TOOLS

Submissions made to forums can usually be seen by everyone because forums (above) and all the postings and responses found there are usually visible to the entire class or all people in a specific group. This visibility is great for workshop submissions and other resources like links to further readings or resources. The VLE might also be set up to include private submissions, usually via an assignment tool, that will go directly from the tutor to the student. Some tutors also ask for submissions via email, but again a benefit of an assignment submission tool on the VLE is that everything you submit is held on the course and easily visible by tutor and student in the context of the course site.

RESOURCES
There are infinite types of resources: from the straightforward links to pdfs or .docs to online resources like *The Guardian* podcasts, *YouTube* or links to resources created by your tutor. Some teachers will provide podcasts or recorded lectures or seminars that you can listen to at your leisure. Or they may invite along visiting speakers to talk to the class or participate in a Q&A session. A course might include recordings of events or visiting speakers to give a fuller experience. The possibilities for resources are nearly endless (although there can be copyright issues with some material) and many classes also carry on additional communications through social media. Although writing is about writing, it's also about art and arts practice, about cultural awareness and context, and when you learn online you can add to and start up these discussions by offering up links that might be of interests to your tutor and your peers. This sort of contributory sharing is crucial to any ongoing discussion and to the sense of community that can build online.

All learning is moving in this multi-media direction. What's quite powerful about this is that as learners we link directly to primary source material and this material can be embedded in docs or websites or VLEs, and this wider scope of reference makes online learning more dynamic. Again, it does take time to access and read/listen/watch this supplementary material and how and where you spend your time is something to consider and plan for.

Webinars

Webinars are becoming more common. They are basically a more advanced type of video-Skype-ing, but where many people can see each other in a virtual 'seminar' space. Webinars can often include document sharing, audio and/or video participation (and often text too, including private discussions) and in the very good systems, these are logged too. So you can hold a full seminar or workshop online, and even gain back some of the things lost through a text based chat or forums – like facial expression and tone of voice.

Wikis

A wiki is an online collaborative too where all students and tutors can contribute and edit text equally. Wikis can be used for practical things such as tutorial or student-led session sign-ups or for creative projects like communally created creative texts.

Invisibility online

If you don't participate in forums and chats, if you don't communicate to your tutor and your classmates, you're invisible online. Some of us are quiet learners, and this can be a difficult learning practice to sustain online. If you have questions, you need to ask them. If you don't ask and problems arise, frustrations build, and the responsibility for this lies with you because a tutor teaching online has many fewer clues to go on about how you're feeling and reacting (face to face, a teacher can see body language, facial response, has more small talk, etc., to get a gauge of how students are doing).

So much of what happens online is via writing. The conversations that often happen in a live classroom, like the ice-breaking or the informal conversations that happen before or after class, are crucial to building the social element of a class. Online small talk serves the same purpose. It's important to remember that it's a community of peers, and we're all responsible for building a rapport in the classroom. This is especially true online. Keep up-to-date with the forums, especially if you miss anything, and make sure you contribute questions and comments because the forums are where a lot of information and a lot of the building of relationships happen.

You need to make your presence known online. Even posting quick messages or questions, like 'Hi, how you doing today? I really enjoyed Sally's comments about John's piece. They made me think about my own character in the short story I'm writing' can be crucial to the flow and vibrancy of a class. Such informal contributions create not only smaller, lighter conversations but also a familiarity that often leads to the more 'meaty' discussions about the craft and graft of writing.

In an online course you do sometimes have to search for the information you need, but if you pay attention, find ways that you can keep track of people and resources, and invest time in creating a strong, approachable online presence, then the course will make day-to-day sense (and become part of your daily writing practice). If you learn to read closely and carefully and are clear in how you communicate by paying attention to meaning and tone, and if you try to invest your writing online (even silly asides and practical messages) with clarity, then you are valuing your own learning and the experience of the class as a whole as well.

Practise your craft

Practise your craft every day, with every message, with every forum post, with every comment. Online learning creates a higher burden of attention to our own words because carelessly written comments or posts can quickly escalate into misunderstanding and defensiveness, both of which bar real learning. The way we write (our writing processes and practices) becomes crucial to how we participate in online environments. The better we understand our own creative practices and needs, our own habits in written communication, the better we can communicate in online forums, and the more you and your peers will learn. Online writing courses often include an element of peer-to-peer feedback, and having some basic grounding in what constitutes good feedback can be very useful.

As students of writing, we should dedicate a lot of time to reading and commenting on the work of our peers. Rather than view this as something that takes you away from your own writing and learning, view all feedback as an opportunity to hone your critical reading skills and your ability

81

to use language well. It is also an opportunity to build commensurate skills such as editing and proofreading.

Online classes are not just about you getting feedback on your writing. It's very useful to see what is said about other pieces and to decide if you agree with the critical comments given. It's crucial to process how you agree with it, and, if you disagree, why you disagree. By reading people's comments or being able to go back to the log of a text-based discussion, you can more carefully see the discussion of a piece, the quality and the type of the feedback given on other people's writing as well as your own. After, you can make decisions about how you can apply that learning about different approaches and criticisms to your own writing.

We're all used to cutting corners or rushing when communicating, especially online. We assume people understand what we intend to mean, and we can be thoughtless in the words we use and how we use them. We tend to post things quickly, without due consideration (the tweet, text or email we wished we hadn't sent!), and this carries particular risks online. An online creative writing course is a great place to practise attention to the words you use, to always comment and respond with consideration of others and to really take the time to become a better writer and communicator.

Language and structure matters

When communicating online, it's good to keep a few things in mind: pay attention to your tone, intention and clarity in all you write online (from forum messages to questions to the feedback you give to your peers). This means that all messages, emails, questions and responses, as well as the work you put up, should be viewed as opportunities to hone your own writing. It's a bit of an inward challenge to keep in mind.

Praise can play an important role in any workshop or classroom situation and even more so online. Remember to be clear and specific with praise, reference specific elements of their work or their comments and build on the critical observations they've offered. Empty praise feels just like that: empty. But genuine and grounded praise, where you've paid attention to a piece or writing or a discussion point, is the building block of strong discussions that then move out into questions and other observations and opinions. Specific praise plays a crucial, underutilised and under-recognised role in effective discussions. When we go to do something quickly, we can forget to notice and mention the strengths of a piece or response, and, as writers, it's crucial to be able to recognise what is working and why so we can build on that in our rewrites and edits.

Thank people for their feedback and responses. If anything struck you as particularly useful, mention it in your reply, again, being specific.

We can get into a critical mode and not only forget to praise but also forget to ask questions. Questioning is at the heart of good creative practice and self-editing. In your responses, give a balance of questions and comments and be aware of how you word opinions and comments.

Questioning works particularly well online because you can build in the time to pay attention to how you phrase questions, to make sure they're open and specific and will be really useful for people to answer. Questions can be fantastic online, in that people can be helped to focus on areas of curiosity and concern. Questions can be clarifying, emerge from curiosity or follow on from other questions or comments and can help shape a fuller, more pertinent discussion.

To summarise, we can use an online creative writing class to become better critical readers, thinkers and responders, and this makes us better writers as we become aware of the necessity of economy in writing, of the needs of an audience, of the usefulness of saying what you mean with clarity and of the essential fact that what you write makes an impact and therefore the tone and approach of your writing matters absolutely. All these skills apply to creative work as well.

More complexly, when we pay attention to language and to how it's used, we start to look at the larger constructions, for instance how to construct messages and comments as a whole, a balance of praise and strengths, questions and opinions. We become aware of how discussions move back and forth as they build into full, useful and enjoyable conversations on the craft and graft of writing. This can help us to understand and to apply larger or more complex structures to our own creative work.

Finally

Here are some basics to keep in mind.

1. Keep a notebook handy, take notes and keep track of things to do, who people are, etc. Don't forget old technologies in the midst of new ones! Use your calendars and notebooks as you normally would, to keep the course and yourself grounded in your everyday life.

2. Keep up to date with all forums and posts. If you get behind, you're more likely to feel out of the loop, confused and frustrated. Staying up to date takes time, so make sure you set aside time to check forums and chats, or add these forums to the list of places you check every day, such as Facebook, Twitter and email.

3. Just because everyone has 24-hour access doesn't mean everyone is online 24 hours a day. Online tools allow us more flexibility in terms of when and how we access and send information, and, when submitting and downloading online, due dates are as important as when you learn face to face. We still need time to do our writing and reading and thinking, and you may find it useful to define the time you spend online. The online environment does provide quicker and more efficient communications, both for distance learning and online support for campus-based courses, and if you realise how you can best use these tools, the better off you'll be.

Overall, pay attention to how you communicate online because there are some things that are particularly problematic. Online we're unable to read facial expressions, body language or silences the way we can in a face-to-face course. And it can be easy to forget that you're missing those clues, or for people to drop out of sight or sound and be absent from the discussions. As a student online, it's important to remember that you need to be present, not just by reading but by contributing online. And not just as a recipient but as an initiator, as someone who asks questions, makes some small talk (help set the tone of an online space) and helps create a sense of a group online by being yourself and finding a way to do this. By paying attention to the words you use and how you use them, you're building critical reading and writing skills, practising your craft and building the online community as well.

A good VLE should be relatively easy to understand but will still take time to become familiar with. Figure out the ways you work online, keep active on the course, ask questions, be aware of the tone and the clarity of everything you write on the course, and, in all messages and postings, be yourself and be present. Learning online takes time, but it's up to you to organise your own schedule and such flexibility suits writing, which is a private, time-consuming, all-hours sort of activity. The online creative writing course can become that too, something you make your own, use it to most help your writing and your writing processes, to find peers, to be useful to them, to enjoy their company and to get the most from your tutors and your peers, so you can improve your own writing.

Chapter Seven

The role of editing and redrafting, and how to do both

Spencer Jordan

Take a deep breath. This may come as something of a shock. That short story you're writing, that novel in the cardboard box under the bed. It'll never be finished or complete. Period. Even when you think you've cracked it, even when you think you couldn't improve a single word or phrase, your writing will remain incomplete. Imperfect.

Apologies if this comes as a shock. This isn't to say that your novel or short story isn't very good. That it isn't ground-breaking and an international best-seller. Rather, it's recognising that anything you write does not have a predetermined 'perfect' state. That 'completion' is something you have to decide yourself, as the writer. What you thought was finished one day becomes incomplete the next. It is this *subjectivity* of editing and revision, the *subjectivity* that surrounds ideas of completion and incompletion, that are at the heart of this chapter.

It's never over till it's over, or the myth of the finished story

Go into a library and pick up any novel or poetry or short story collection. Look at the name on the front, then flick through the pages. I can see you reading the odd sentence, looking again at the front cover. You want to sit down and read it, disappear into its world. Yet the book you've chosen is something else as well. It's the end product of countless drafts and revisions, a hidden, forgotten process that perhaps took place over many months or even years. Not that you'd know that from the book in your hand. Like a bad dream, the agony of redrafting has been exorcised. All we've got as readers is the final polished text. So, here's our first problem: revision and editing tends to be invisible; the creative practice that 'dare not speak its name'.

Some famous authors whose work was heavily edited include:

- James Joyce, *Ulysses* (1922)
- J. R. R. Tolkien, *The hobbit* (1937)
- Raymond Carver, *What we talk about when we talk about love* (1981)

Writers tend to keep quiet about the amount of editing and revising they do, as though it's an admission of weakness that their novel or short story didn't come in one blinding flash of inspiration. It's this romanticised notion of writing that is the problem here. We still like to project the idea that our work comes from some secret creative spring, ready-made and fully formed. The concept that writing needs to be crafted, and then edited, and then edited again, that the creative journey involves cul-de-sacs and dead ends, is out of kilter with how we like to project ourselves as writers.

The reality of writing, however, is this: a novel or short story can go through hundreds, if not thousands, of edits and redrafts. Charles Dickens edited his work, as did James Joyce. We know because we still have the original manuscripts where we can actually see their pen-written deletions and insertions. Even writers whose works have been published find themselves returning to their manuscript, tinkering, or even making dramatic changes. A good example is J. R. R. Tolkien. As he began work on *The lord of the rings* (1954), Tolkien realised he needed to make some significant changes to the original version of *The hobbit* (1937), in particular altering Gollum's relationship to the One Ring. This second edition was published in 1951; a third edition, with further edits, was published in 1966.

Even if you're happy with the text, you may find that an editor still insists on changes. This was the case with the short story writer Raymond Carver whose early work was heavily revised by his editor at Alfred A. Knopf. It's now possible to read both the published *and* manuscript versions of his collection, *What we talk about when we talk about love* (1981), in *Collected stories* (2009).

There seems to be a clear message here. If revision and editing are good enough for Dickens, Joyce, Tolkien and Carver, some of the most influential and successful writers in the English language, perhaps we should look more closely at what editing and revision can give us. We've already seen that, unlike a building which is constructed with clear plans, costs and prior agreements, your own writing is open-ended. Calling it 'finished' is your shout, a subjective one, sometimes based more on pragmatic issues such as time and exhaustion than on any instinct you might have about the completeness of the work. James Joyce famously gave himself just such a pragmatic completion date for *Ulysses*: 2 February 1922, his fortieth birthday. Without it he could easily have spent a lifetime lost in the labyrinth of one of literature's most complicated novels. But don't panic. This chapter is all about how you can come to terms with this phenomenon and about the techniques you can use to make editing and redrafting work for you.

Here we go again: editing and redrafting, the key techniques

One of the most important things to take away from this chapter is that editing is an *integral* part of the creative writing process. It certainly should not be seen as something separate from it, a voluntary activity for the deluded, that you can take or leave, depending on how much time and energy you have.

> Remember, a good author doesn't just write. They are:
> - writer
> - reader
> - editor
>
> all rolled into one. And they make the tea.

Successful writers tend to be those who recognise the importance of revision. For them, the penny has dropped that creative writing isn't limited to the first raw draft but instead percolates down through subsequent revisions. A good analogy is that of the film director: the film isn't made by the raw footage shot in the studio but is instead created in the darkness of the editing suite, long after the actors have gone, when the hundreds of feet of film are cut and spliced together to create a story. You may not have thought of it before but, when you're editing your writing, you're Steven Spielberg or Quentin Tarantino.

In particular, editing is vital to short story, poetry and flash-fiction writing. In these forms, when space and technique are at a premium, editing your work becomes even more important. In the longer form of novels, editing is needed to ensure the consistency of the story. In these instances, editing should be seen as just another part of the writing process.

If you want to be a consistent writer of high-quality fiction, then it simply won't be good enough to be a great writer of amazing first drafts. As this section has argued, you'll need two other skills as well: you will need to be a good, *critical* reader of your own work and you will need to be a confident, and brave, editor of your work, a writer who's not afraid to roll up their sleeves and undertake sometimes significant and, let's be honest, painful, redrafting.

In summary then, a good author is these three things: *writer, reader, editor*, all rolled into one. And it is these skills that form that basis of good editing and revision.

So, who exactly does this editing?

This might seem a silly question. Surely it's the writer, *you*, who edits. And, of course, that's true. Up to a point. After all, it'll be you who'll be reading and editing your work as you write. It'll be you with that film director's cap on, controlling and manipulating the text. Yet it's also important to bear in mind that, at key moments in the writing process, people other than you *could* be involved. The creative act itself is very often a private, personal affair.

A process cut off from the outside world. And that's fine. Yet, when it comes to editing what you've written, different rules apply. Editing can be understood far more as a *shared* activity, one in which the writer might even take the back seat. To the benefit of the text.

So, who are these people?

A friend or 'trusted reader'

OK, this is the situation. You've just finished a complete first draft of your short story or novel. You're really pleased with it. Who wouldn't be? But what should you do next? Should you send it to an agent, a publisher? Hide it under the bed and start something new? The answer is none of these. Instead, the best advice to a writer at this point, when they have a good first draft in their hands, is that it's time to hand it over to someone else to read. A second pair of eyes, but, most importantly, a pair you can *trust*.

The word *trust* is important. The person you select should be someone you think will be fair and as unbiased in their assessment of your work as possible. This may seem easy, but actually it's often a bit more difficult than it looks. For example, a close friend might seem a good choice. Perhaps they've read some of your writing before. And they owe you a favour or two. But think again. Will they be too keen to shower you with compliments rather than engage *critically* with the writing? They're your friend after all, of course they're going to say that they love your writing. Aren't they?

What you're really looking for is someone you can trust to say when things are good but also someone who will have the confidence to voice any concerns they have *fairly*, perhaps about the plot, or your characterisation, for example. As a writer, someone who is perhaps exposing their work for the first time, you need to be able to trust that these critical comments are being made honestly and in good faith and not because the person you've asked holds a personal grudge against you.

So, who can you ask? Well, only you can answer that. But here are a few basic ground rules which will certainly help you:

Checklist for a friend or trusted reader

1. Are they as close as possible to your 'intended reader'?
2. Have you thought about which parts of your novel or story to give them?
3. Have you specific questions you'd like your reader to answer?

The first thing to consider is that the person you pick should be as close as possible to the *ideal* or *intended* reader for your work as possible. What this means is that if you're writing a chick-lit novel, one that will have particular appeal to young single women, for example, the person you ask to read your draft should represent your intended readership. Your brother, uncle or dad, for example, might not be best placed to offer their views, no matter how well intentioned they are. If your writing doesn't have an easily identifiable reader, you should pick someone who enjoys reading, whom you could imagine buying your work if it were for sale in a bookshop.

The second point refers specifically to those who have written a novel. Do not give your trusted reader the entire manuscript. More than likely it will overwhelm them, and they'll just skim through it. So, instead, offer them just the first three chapters or some other manageable portion from the beginning of the novel. And when they've read that, ask them if they would like a few more chapters. And after that, a few more, and so on. That way, you won't overwhelm them. Importantly, however, it will still allow you to ask their opinions as they're progressing through the story, section by section. If you're clever you can then capture their views at key stages of the narrative. From the writer's perspective, this might be important in terms of understanding if the reader has grasped plot or character development, for instance. It will also indicate whether or not your readers want to continue reading it.

Whether you're writing a novel or a short story, it can sometimes be useful to give your 'trusted reader' a number of specific questions you want them to address or comment on. This can be very useful for a number of reasons. First, it offers your reader a framework. Without it, they may feel rather lost. Just telling them to read your story, saying whether they like it or not, might leave them floundering. What are they actually meant to say? At best, the feedback you get will be unfocused and overgeneralised; at worst, it will be practically valueless.

Instead, give your reader three or four areas you'd like them to comment on explicitly. For example, you might ask them about the plot. Perhaps you might also ask them for comments on a particular character. These questions could be very general, or you might ask something with a very specific focus: 'What was your reaction to the murder of character X?' 'Did you find the ending of Chapter 5 believable?' And so on. But don't give your trusted reader *too* many questions. I would suggest five at most. And make sure they're the questions that you really want to ask. This means you need to sit down and think carefully about them before you start handing out your work for comment. Where are you unsure about the writing, where would a second pair of eyes really help?

An editor or agent

It's important to bear in mind that even when you think the novel or short story you're writing is as finished and complete as it can be, it may well be required to go through a *further* stage of editing and redrafting. For example, if an agent accepts your manuscript, he or she may well do so on condition that you make a number of revisions and changes to the text. The agent is doing this because they think that your manuscript will be more marketable to a publisher with those changes. These edits could be uncontroversial and something you're willing to do. But they could also be more significant. Perhaps the agent wishes to change the ending, or to cut out key chapters. In this instance, you'll need to discuss the edits carefully with the agent. You might be persuaded that the edits are for the best, or you might seek to negotiate a compromise. There's no hard and fast rule here I'm afraid. However, I would say that if your relationship with an agent is going to succeed it must be based on trust. Rejecting an agent's suggestions out of hand might be the correct decision. Or, more plausibly, it might indicate a writer who has become too blinkered and 'precious' about their own writing.

The same applies to an editor. When your work is finally accepted by a publisher, an editor could very well insist on further edits and revisions before publication. We've seen this already with Raymond Carver, for instance. Another example is *Lord of the flies* (1954), William Golding's first novel. The editor, Charles Monteith, pruned a number of sections, and he didn't like Golding's original title either, *Strangers from within*. The rest, as they say, is history.

Editing that you can do

Having looked at using friends as editors, and the role of professional agents and editors, it's time we returned to the one person who will be doing the vast majority of the editing on your work: you. As the writer, the editing will be your primary responsibility. A lot of the editing you'll undertake will be done before anyone else gets a chance to look at the text.

From the writer's perspective, there are two basic types of editing: what I will term *ongoing editing* and *summative editing*.

ONGOING EDITING

Ongoing editing is editing as you write.

Focus on

- spelling
- vocabulary
- syntax (sentence structure)

You might not realise it, but as you write, word by word, sentence by sentence, you are constantly editing your work. As you finish a sentence, for example, it's almost impossible not to quickly read it through, changing the odd word perhaps, adding a comma or two, before moving on to the next sentence. Word processors make this *ongoing* editing easier than it used to be. With pen and paper, any edits had to be written alongside the existing sentence, perhaps in the margin, or else the entire sentence or paragraph would have to be laboriously rewritten. You can see this on the handwritten manuscripts of many famous novels. It's something all writers do instinctively. It's almost a reflex action, so intimately connected with the writing process that you hardly realise you're doing it.

The key things to concentrate on at this stage are threefold:

1. **Spelling.** Never, ever, submit a manuscript to an agent or publisher that has not been vigorously checked and rechecked for mistakes. Although some recommend leaving spelling mistakes until the final draft, I would recommend that you correct misspellings as you go along, right from the first draft. This will make work simpler in the long run. Trying to correct misspellings in a completed story is far harder and requires lots more concentration that doing it as you go along. Believe me.
2. **Vocabulary.** Think carefully about your vocabulary as you are writing. Often we use the first words we think of, plucked from a small pool of words we feel comfortable with. Stretch yourself, use a thesaurus, especially with adjectives and adverbs. And, the golden rule, avoid clichés. Nothing switches a reader off quicker.

3. **Syntax.** Deciding on appropriate syntax, or sentence structure, is a key part of writing. The first time we write a sentence, we might not get the syntax right.

SYNTAX

First version

The man opened the door and walked into the room he didn't really know what to expect.

Second version

The man opened the door and walked into the room. He didn't really know what to expect.

Third version

The man opened the door. He didn't know what to expect. He walked cautiously into the room.

In the example here we can see that in the first version the writer hasn't got the syntax right at all. The second version corrects this, making the final clause a separate sentence (a comma would have been another option). However, in the third version, the writer has been more ambitious, breaking the original line into three separate sentences and then changing their order (adding the adverb 'cautiously' as he did so). Hopefully you can see that one of the most important aspects of syntax is *rhythm*, how the sentences 'sound' when you read them. The rhythm of those short punchy sentences in version three really heightens the anticipation, drawing the reader into the action.

Let's look a bit more closely at an example of ongoing editing.

> **ONGOING EDITING: AN EXAMPLE**
>
> **First draft**
>
> She shook her head, she was being silly. Gossip is just what the grown-ups do when they are bored.
> She held her breath when she pushed open the door and peered within. It was dark, but he had always liked it like that, it was more fun so she tiptoed through.
>
> **Second draft (with changes marked)**
>
> She shook her head, she was being silly. Gossip<u>ing</u> is just what the grown-ups do when ~~they are~~ bored, <u>everyone knew that</u>.
> Still, she held her breath when she pushed open the door ~~and peered within~~. <u>Inside</u> ~~It~~ was dark, but he'<u>d</u> ~~had~~ always liked it like that, it was more fun ~~so~~<u>.</u> She tiptoed through.
>
> **Final draft**
>
> She shook her head, she was being silly. Gossiping is just what grown-ups do when bored, everyone knew that.
> Still, she held her breath when she pushed open the door. Inside was dark, but he'd always liked it like that, it was more fun. She tiptoed through.

Notice the difference in the writer's work, from the first draft to the 'final' version. The writer is using *free indirect style*, not an easy technique. Reading back her sentences immediately after writing them, she's spotted a few inconsistencies, particularly in syntax. She's slightly overwritten

99

some of the sentences, but she also decides to add 'everyone knew that', to help with the free indirect style. Finally she restructures the second paragraph to help with the rhythm of the piece, before moving on with the rest of her writing.

SUMMATIVE EDITING

The strength of ongoing editing is that it's barely separate from the creative process itself. However, this is also a weakness. A form of editing that is so reflexive, so piecemeal in its approach, means that a more substantial, prolonged and deeper review of the text is necessary at key moments in the lifespan of your writing. Crucially, you need to be able to identify when this more sustained approach to editing is necessary. For this reason, I've called this *summative* editing (editing that occurs at the end of a longer period of writing).

There are two basic modes of summative editing:
1. the 'short and sweet' mode
2. the 'long and hard' mode.

The 'short and sweet' mode
In this mode, a few minutes are set aside to read a preceding chapter, or several pages or paragraphs.

Focus on

- recent plot developments
- dialogue
- pace
- tone

This technique is useful in terms of familiarising yourself with recent plot developments, dialogue, pace and tone. It is often used just before you begin writing for the day, helping you to remember what has been written the day before, thereby maintaining continuity of story, style and pace.

The 'long and hard' mode

In this mode you set aside several hours, perhaps even whole days in the case of a novel, to read the complete work as it currently stands. This is done at key times during the writing, perhaps after the completion of a section or a significant chapter. In this mode, it is important to go right back to the beginning of the story and read everything.

Why do you need to do this? Well, often your own understanding of what has happened in your story loses clarity as you write. Over a period of weeks, months, even years, you can forget scenes and drop ideas or even characters. The writing can also lose tone and consistency of theme. Rereading your writing from the very beginning, whether it's a short story or novel, will help you avoid all of these things.

But be warned. This longer form of editing is the hardest to do, yet it is the most important. To help, here are some tips to make it work for you.

1. Summative editing works best when you can achieve a 'critical distance' from your own writing. Leaving your writing for a few days (or even weeks) is a useful tip here, allowing you to see your writing with 'fresh eyes'.

2. You should be prepared to undertake a close, critical reading of your work. Do not read your work too quickly or superficially. Listen to your instincts as you're reading. They're often right. A sentence which seems a bit too complex probably is and should be changed. A description over which you keep pausing should be changed.
3. However, beware. This sort of critical reading requires high levels of concentration and energy. You should be at your best. A hangover is not a good idea.
4. Always save earlier versions of your work. Never put yourself in a position where you've irrevocably lost any of your writing. You never know when you might need it further down the line. Remember, editing is not just about removing text, it can also be about restoring text which was removed by an earlier edit. If you don't save earlier versions, you won't be able to do this.
5. It can often be useful to set out clear criteria for your summative editing before you begin. Perhaps you recognise a need to concentrate specifically on the plot of your story, or the dialogue of your characters. Or perhaps it's something else. But being truthful and honest about possible weaknesses in your writing, and then using summative editing to help decide whether those weaknesses actually exist (and then removing them) is one excellent way to make editing work for you.
6. Lastly, *be brave*. Be prepared to make those big decisions. As William Faulkner famously said, be prepared to 'kill your darlings'. In other words, every writer should be ready to remove the most dearly loved section of their writing. Cutting large chunks of writing can be painful but is a key part of self-editing. Be ready to see the plot undergo dramatic change.

Stylistic changes, such as altering the perspective from third to first person, as in the case of Salman Rushdie's *Midnight's children* (1981), might be a hard but ultimately correct decision. Being able to face these editorial challenges head on and have your writing come through even stronger and more confident at the end is a key part of the creative process.

Things to remember:
- Get a 'critical distance'
- Listen to your instincts
- Maintain high energy levels
- Save all versions
- Establish criteria
- Be brave

Here's an example of some summative editing.

SUMMATIVE EDITING: AN EXAMPLE
First draft

She shook her head, she was being silly. Gossiping is just what grown-ups do when bored, everyone knew that.

Still, she held her breath when she pushed open the door. Inside was dark, but he'd always liked it like that, it was more fun. She tiptoed through.

Final draft

I shook my head. I knew I was being stupid. Gossiping is just what grown-ups do when bored, everyone knew that. Even Jamie.

> Even so, I couldn't help holding my breath when I finally found the courage to open the door. Inside was dark, but Jamie had always liked it like that. It was more fun, he said. I tiptoed forwards, quietly calling out his name.

Notice how the writer has now made some quite drastic changes. Having finished the story, she's finally realised that free indirect style is not appropriate. So she's changed the entire piece to *first person*. The focus of the scene is now far more about the narrator's relationship with the character called Jamie, a consequence of the writer being aware of what the story is and how it will progress. The darkened room is clearly a powerful metaphor in terms of this relationship and the story's underlying theme. The writing maintains a level of suspense that draws the reader into the scene.

Conclusion

Hopefully what you've learned from this chapter is that editing and revision are an integral part of creative writing. I've suggested a number of key approaches you can use when editing your work. Most of all, I hope this chapter has convinced you that quality writing is made in the editing process and that the best writers are often the bravest when it comes to looking again at their work.

Chapter Eight

Reading aloud: making the most of your work when you present it

Nabila Jameel

If you are taking a degree course in creative writing, the chances are you have already recognised the importance of perfecting the craft of writing, but have you ever considered how vital it is to read well? There is a lot of competition out there, and, unless you are already published, you are unlikely to make many sales. You must take your work out there to an audience.

There is nothing scarier than walking onto a stage in a room full of strange faces and performing a piece of your writing. I have done it: it was a nerve-racking experience, but once I did it and overcame stage fight I became addicted to the buzz that I felt when I made contact with my audience. In this chapter, I hope to explain why it is important to read well and how you can become a more confident reader and performer of your own work.

Later in the chapter, you will read extracts by four writers who specialise in different genres (the novel, scriptwriting, poetry and the short story), which offer their insights into how to approach reading aloud.

The basics

UNDERSTANDING VOICE

Speaking is a beautifully complex process, and much of the time we take this for granted. We can train ourselves to improve the quality of our voice and our ability to project it to fit the purpose, as Michelle Green indicates later in this chapter, but the underlying process of sound production works as follows: air pressure from the lungs creates a flow of air through the trachea (windpipe), larynx (voice box) and pharynx (back of the throat). The folds in the larynx vibrate, creating fluctuations in air pressure that are called sound waves. Resonance in the vocal tract modifies these waves depending on the position and shape of the lips, jaw, tongue, soft palate and other speech organs, creating different qualities of sound. Mouth and nose openings radiate the sound waves into the environment.

Now try speaking while simultaneously thinking about this process by which we make sound. Try to locate the various organs mentioned. You will notice that when you fill your lungs with air and breathe out slowly you can make your voice louder and project it further. The voice should emerge from deep within, not from the throat or upper chest.

AWARENESS OF BODY LANGUAGE

Remember that your audience will be looking at you while you are reading. Try to look confident: avoid habits such as swaying, playing with your hair and twitching. Watch others read and also record and watch yourself. Try to avoid reading from large sheets of paper that get in the way and spoil the flow of the reading. Memorise your work in advance so you can concentrate more on engaging with your audience, then practise reading it aloud in front of a mirror.

Here are some helpful tips that I have picked up over the years, which can significantly improve your reading. Try to make an hour of quiet time each week. You will need a microphone, computer or a dictaphone. Learn a relaxation exercise to help you breathe better and to keep your nerves at bay (a short walk or a ten-minute yoga exercise will also help to clear up the airways for easier breathing). Concentrate on your breathing and try to open up your diaphragm. The voice should come from the deeper, lower part of your chest. Before you attempt to record yourself, memorise two sections of your writing that should each last five minutes. Now record yourself performing these. It is a good idea to record two very different pieces of writing in terms of subject matter. Concentrate on the sound of each word while recording.

When you have finished, play back the recordings and listen to them. You should be able to assess how close or how far you need to be from the microphone in future, depending on how quiet your voice is. Keep a pen and paper handy to make notes on what you think you need to change. Does this performance convey the message you intend to get across to an audience? Are you communicating the emotions well?

Get into the habit of reading in front of a mirror. Ask someone to listen to and watch you read for honest and constructive feedback and ask your observer to pinpoint specifically any habits in your reading which can be irritating for the audience to see, such as swaying from side to side or fidgeting. Try to avoid them.

When are you likely to have to perform your writing?

DURING THE COURSE

You will be sometimes asked to read your work aloud in writing workshops. Knowing how to project the voice, the way you intended to when you wrote it, is vital. Intonation, pause and volume all contribute to a good reading. You wrote it, and only you know what you intended to say through it, so make sure you communicate the right message using your voice in the most effective and appropriate way.

Practise reading other people's work in order to develop different reading styles.

SETTING UP YOUR OWN STUDENT PERFORMANCE GROUP

At university, it will look great on your CV if you set up your own performance group or coordinated one with someone else. Performance groups are exceptionally useful for those who feel shy about performing or who are anxious about reading to a crowd. You are with people you know in a warm, relaxed environment from which you can slowly grow before entering a space outside the university. Most creative writing departments are supportive of this and offer a venue for such a group to meet.

AUDIO-VISUAL

It is becoming very common for writers to produce audio-visual recordings of their work. Take a look at the Poetry Channel. You may want to have a go at making your own film, alone or in collaboration with someone else.

I worked in collaboration with a film-maker and produced a poetry-film, which came about after I submitted a poem to Comma Press. Comma Press is a publisher based in Manchester that runs an annual Comma Film challenge to which film-makers and writers are invited to submit their work. Film-makers are invited to create films from submitted poems and short stories. The films are then screened, judged by a panel, and the best one wins. You'll find a link below to the film based on my poem.[1] My poem was selected by a film-maker who produced a short film based on her own interpretation of my words. I sent her a sound recording of the poem in my own voice. This was a hugely valuable experience for me through which I clearly saw the strengths and weaknesses of my physical voice. Learning to let go of my child (the poem) was difficult. However, for me, the greatest benefit of this exercise was the availability of the film online – it gave me exposure.

If you are a scriptwriter, you could also find yourself having to deliver your script aloud in a script reading, so knowing how your voice projects, how it bounces and what tone it carries is important in this context too. You would have to pay particular attention to the characters in the script and how they would sound.

Take a look at some of Daljit Nagra's and John Cooper Clarke's performances on YouTube to see how powerfully they read their poetry. I like these in particular:

Daljit Nagra ('This be the pukka verse')
　　www.youtube.com/watch?feature=endscreen&NR=1&v=TupeT4c8F_o

---

[1] Here is a link to the film based on my poem, 'Until next time': http://movingpoems.com/2010/10/until-next-time-by-nabila-jameel

John Cooper Clarke ('Beasley Street')
www.youtube.com/watch?v=euD0o0x-jAo

Notice how different their styles are, especially as John Cooper Clarke has music to accompany his piece. Focus on their body language, their emphasis on key words that bring the poems to life and the contrast between their quiet mutters and loud outbursts. Although Nagra is reading from a sheet, he does not rely solely on this. He often looks away from the page towards the camera, and this makes us feel we are in the room with him. Clarke knows his poetry by heart as he is a performance poet, so is used to having to do this, but both are effective readers. Why? Because they captivate us and hold our attention. This takes time and years of practice.

For genres such as drama, short story or indeed prose in general you can listen to radio programmes to learn about voice and technique. In the UK, programmes such as BBC Radio 4's *Poetry please*, *Afternoon reading* and *15 minute drama* are all very good. Sometimes, seeing a written piece detracts from the feel you get from the sound alone. So, if your interest is more in sound rather than visuals, try to listen to recordings of the written word.

Using social media: Facebook, Twitter and blogs

How do you promote your work while you are studying or after you have graduated? Many writers now use social media to get their work out there. You may want to produce a sound recording with an image and post it to Twitter, Facebook or a personal blog. This draws more attention to the words, as there are no moving images or text. If you have not already tried attaching an audio link to your work from a social-media site, view this as an experiment that could lead to more opportunities. Those who follow you will want to know more about your work, and any comments you receive will be an indication of whether it is of a good standard and whether it achieves its objectives. Are people's responses what you expected them to be? If not, do not be offended. Take any comments on board and reflect on them. Remember, these people are your audience and you are writing for them, so value what they say. If we publish our work on the Internet we should be willing to accept criticism. Slowly, with time, you will develop an extra layer of skin!

Slam performances

Slams are competitions at which writers read or recite original work. These performances are then judged on a numeric scale by previously selected members of the audience, and the person with the most points wins.

Poetry slams are the most common, but there are also slams for other types of writing, such as non-fiction and flash fiction. There are slam poets performing all over the country. Performance poets rely very little, if at all, on paper. You may become involved in a performance group. It is highly competitive but worth it to get to a few slam shows to see what skills you can pick up. Remember you can learn a lot by simply observing and listening. Slam poets are undoubtedly good wordsmiths but are often undervalued or even dismissed by academics. This is mainly because they were regarded as less technically sound on paper. So keep an open mind and explore this area: it is an opportunity to network too, so you have nothing to lose!

Marketing

When your first book is published, whether it is a novel, a volume of poetry or part of an anthology, it is likely that you will be required to take an active role in marketing it. Depending on the publisher, this will involve you attending launch events at local or national level. These could take place at libraries or bookshops. People will come to listen with the intention of buying the book. If they hear extracts from the book read by the author, they are more likely to buy it. You must be able to read with confidence. Writing is a business at the end of the day, and the better you are at this side of the business the greater the chances of the book being sold.

You could also be asked to read and discuss your work on radio, in which case you need to speak with a clear voice and appropriate tone.

Careers

'There are various alternative careers where being able to speak clearly and confidently is crucial. For example, if you decide to teach creative writing after completing the course, you must be able to read well and to be able to deliver lectures and seminars. Refining your voice will enable you to communicate more effectively with your students. Alternatively, you may decide to pursue a career in publishing. This will involve speaking at public events and representing an author.

Writers' opinions

I asked a few writers why they thought it was important to be able to read well and to suggest techniques that they use to perform at their best. They speak from their own experience.

Here is what Nicholas Royle, a well-known British writer, had to say:

> It's vitally important to be able to read well when reading your work in public. An author can breathe life into their work at a reading. Equally, they can kill it stone dead. It's really the only chance you have – apart from on the page – to communicate to the world what your work means to you, and a good reading can make all the difference. The best advice is to keep it short and to make sure you've rehearsed. Don't go on stage and read your work aloud if you haven't already done exactly that at home. Of course, you should have read it aloud before submitting it anywhere, but it's always a good idea to have another run-through, especially if reading from a published text. You never know what little mistakes might have crept in.

Michelle Green is a poet and short story writer and an excellent performer, based in the UK. She taught me many things about technique when I attended some of her classes on performance. Here she elaborates on some of the points I made earlier. The links mentioned towards the end of her piece are particularly useful.

> A live reading is different from the one-on-one interior experience of a reader and a book. It is communal and ephemeral; it

offers a chance for the sounds and rhythms of writing to take flight. In practical terms, performance also means exposure: to readers, other writers and literature-development folk. Live events are good for promoting work, whether it's published or not, and if you are published they are great places to sell books: copies of my poetry collection have almost exclusively sold at readings and performances. The key to delivering a quality performance is preparation. A poorly adjusted microphone, crumpled paper held up in front of the face, a mumbled or whispered delivery, lack of eye contact with the audience, monotone delivery or, even worse, a contrived and puffed-up 'performance voice' that barrels over all nuance in the writing – all of these can destroy a piece of writing and leave the audience stone cold. Here are a few tips harvested from my experience, and some useful links below.

Well before a live event: find out how much time you've got and time your material accordingly. Read it aloud several times at least so you can hear how it sounds. If you find yourself rushing or getting breathless, mark on the page the places where you will take a breath. Face the wall when you read aloud, about two feet away, so you can hear your own voice bounce back. Practise the vocal exercises on the Voice Guy website (see link below) to help strengthen your voice. Know your work inside and out, so the page is there as a guide, not a crutch.

Decide on a short introduction to each piece so that you don't end up rambling on for five minutes before getting down to reading your poem or story. If you don't want to use intros, then plan the silent spaces between your pieces and hold onto them. Immediately before a live reading or performance, warm up your voice by humming. Yawn deeply a few times; this releases tension in your throat and improves your alertness by getting more oxygen to your brain. Take a few slow, deep breaths. Breathe so that your lower abdomen moves out on the in-breath.

While reading and performing, either use the microphone or move it out of your way. Make any necessary adjustments before you start your reading, and once you begin don't touch it. Each little touch of the mic and stand sounds like a rock falling down the stairs, so just leave it alone. If the stand needs adjusting and you don't know how, ask the event host or stage tech to do it for you. Breathe. Breathe again.

S-L-O-W D-O-W-N. It might sound too slow in your head, but that's not how it sounds to an audience who have never heard your piece before. Give them time to take the words in. Hold your page or book no higher than elbow height and look down with your eyes, not your whole face. If you're familiar with your material you shouldn't need to read word for word. If you lose your place or make a mistake, just stop, take a second to find your place, and then start again. You don't need to apologise or think that you've ruined the reading. You haven't. Make eye contact with the audience regularly. Plan this beforehand if you need to. *Think about what you are saying as you say it.* Feel what you are saying. This will keep the words fresh and meaningful and will help you connect with the audience. When the audience applauds, take a moment to accept it.

Useful web links

The Voice Guy
http://voiceguy.ca/the-warm-up-series
This has lots of good vocal exercises to get your voice and breathing in shape, with audio tracks as well as text.

> **How to give a good reading of your poems**
> http://poetry.about.com/od/livepoetry/ht/howgivereading.htm
> Taken from Gary Mex Glazner's book *How to make a living as a poet*. Poet-focused but applicable to all creative writing forms.
> **Performance poetry guide**
> http://applesandsnakes.org/page/3612/Performance+Poetry+Guide
> Again this is written with performance poetry in mind, but there are good tips in there for live literature.
> **Suheir Hammad, Def Poetry**
> http://youtu.be/0fhWX2F6G7Y
> Palestinian–American poet Suheir Hammad shows how to give a powerful reading with paper in hand of her piece 'First Writing Since'.

Peter Kalu is the creative director of Commonword (a writing development organisation and publisher) in Manchester and a scriptwriter. He gives the following advice:

> I began as a poet and grew into writing novels and scripts for theatre, radio and screen. I have found reading drama scripts a great way of reaching an audience and getting them enthused about my writing. I have visited a number of prisons (by invitation I should add!). A significant number of prisoners cannot read. Many of them are also excellent raconteurs. So to tell them a story is to enter a world of experts in many respects. When I read scripts in prisons, I give a basic overview of my script: the bare bones of the plot, the theme I might be exploring and who the characters are. Then I read an extract. I like to read with passion and to enjoy the reading of the script myself as much

> as I enjoyed writing it initially. It is that passion and enjoyment that is infectious and that engages the audience. Usually, if I have inspired them sufficiently, some of those who are literate will want to read parts themselves. If all goes according to plan, I can simply sit and listen to them. I have heard some great readings of my scripts, with improvisations, sound effects and spot-on dialects thrown in spontaneously by the prisoners.
>
> Any script I read aloud I have usually read several times in advance to make sure that I am not going to stumble over any words and I can look up at the audience rather than mumbling into my sheet of papers. I try to choose scripts that suit the anticipated audience. So, for a culturally diverse audience, I take scripts or material that reflect this diversity – that way everyone has an entry point. Time of day and age range of the audience are also factors.

You can see here that Peter often reads in an environment where the audience is made up of good listeners. They are probably more alert to the way he projects his voice than the average person.

Ben Mellor is a poet and experienced performer. He won the 2009 BBC Radio 4 National Poetry Slam. He says:

> I began taking acting seriously from about the age of thirteen, the same age I started writing poetry and songs. Although I sang my lyrics fronting a teenage grunge band, it wasn't until I got to university that I started speaking my poetry to audiences without the protection of thrashing guitars and crashing drums to close my eyes and bang my head against so I couldn't see the audience.
>
> Taking to the stage on my own to perform poetry was certainly easier having had the experience of being in plays and

leaping about with a band. However, in both those instances you are playing a character to some extent. It's harder when you have to be yourself, which is probably why a lot of my poetry was, and still is, character-based. You have a metaphorical mask to hide behind, and your perceptions of the audience's judgements can be deflected by it to a degree.

I've always struggled more with the bits in-between, introducing myself and my work whilst trying to project a witty, affable and relaxed persona. But as time has gone on I've found that easier; I'm more comfortable and less nervous. I suppose that's my first, and not very helpful, lesson: public speaking gets easier the more you do it. That said, I know some poets who meticulously script all their links and perform them with the same fidelity as they do their poems, whilst all the time seeming to be spontaneously witty and urbane. So if you have a fear of improvising you could try writing down everything you'll say, even the asides, and learning them.

Then comes the danger of word or, more properly, image fatigue. This is the autopilot problem; when you've learned what you're going to say so well and repeated it so often that you don't see the pictures in your mind any more and the words fall dead off your tongue. This is probably more important in theatre and poetry than it might be in, say, giving a business presentation. But the fact remains that if you don't visualise what you're saying as you say it, and thereby maintain your emotional connection to your words, then your audience won't connect with it either.

You may not think that there are many emotions inherent in delivering a report in a boardroom or presenting a paper in a seminar for instance, but, as with any public speaking, you are trying to convince an audience of something, even if that's just that they should be paying attention. To pay attention they must be excited and interested in what you're saying, which means you must be too. Having an emotional connection to your material will mean that you can reflect that in the pitch and tone, providing a rich vocal landscape of hills and valleys rather than a flat, monotonous fenland.

But don't assume that your audience doesn't want to be excited and interested in what you're saying either. A lot of our nervousness around public speaking arises from projecting our insecurities onto the crowd and having it reflected back as assumed hostility. A clichéd bit of advice to public speakers to make them feel they have one up on their audience is to imagine them naked, the idea being I suppose that you reduce everyone down to a basic human level and they seem less intimidating. However, I do not particularly find the thought of a bunch of naked people staring at you any less intimidating, just a bit disturbing and rather distracting. I think the thing to remember is that in the vast majority of cases the people you are speaking to want you to be good, want you to succeed. Not in a 'we'll throw things at you if you don't' kind of way, but just in a gentle, supportive, 'we'd be just as nervous if we were in your shoes' kind of way.

Another bit of advice commonly given to first-time speakers is to avoid having to make eye contact by speaking at a point just over people's heads. This may be useful if you find yourself terminally unable to lift your face from the page but if you never make eye contact, you risk your words, well, going over peoples' heads. It can be hard making eye contact at first; it can feel challenging and uncomfortable. Again, and in a similarly unhelpful 'no shortcuts' vein, it gets easier with practice.

I once met a t'ai chi teacher who never made eye contact with people because he believed the energy exchanged was so powerful. I understand what he meant, but it did make him very difficult to communicate with. I think that eye contact is essential

> to convey what you're trying to say to people. If you make eye contact with as many people as you can in the crowd (provided that the lights aren't so bright as to make them invisible), even for the most fleeting of moments, then everyone will feel as if you've spoken directly to them.
>
> I enter a lot of poetry slams, where audience members or a panel of judges give you a score after you've performed. If I didn't make a lot of eye contact I wouldn't be able to transmit the way I feel about what I'm saying, and the judges wouldn't feel moved to give me many points. Unless you also enter slams, you won't have to suffer the discomfort of someone putting a numerical value on your performance, but the more eye contact you can make with individual members of your audience, the better what you're saying will be received by them as a whole.

Ben's reference to imagining people naked made me laugh. Someone once told me to do this but it just made me more nervous. However, it works for some people! Finally, some advice from British novelist Rachel Connor:

> As someone who used to lecture for a living, I'm no stranger to reading aloud. I know the importance of a well-structured talk, of projecting the voice and sustaining eye contact. It's much more difficult to remember all this, though, when it's my own words, not someone else's, that I'm faced with. There's a danger that when I'm more emotionally invested in the writing, I'm less mindful about delivery. When my debut novel, *Sisterwives*, was published in October 2011, I not only had to reacquaint myself with the techniques of public speaking, I had to think for the first time about my persona as an author.
>
> One thing I do know is this: reading well is vital in building a readership. Every reading is a sales pitch. And I don't simply

mean that it sells books (though, done well, it can do that too). It's about persuading readers to see what you see, about putting across your message with passion and verve. Isn't this why we write in the first place? I found myself returning to the fundamentals and working out why I wanted to write the novel in the first place. I doodled and mind-mapped until I'd got to grips with the essential messages I wanted *Sisterwives* to convey.

I'm fortunate to work for the UK's Arvon Foundation, which runs residential courses in the UK for aspiring writers, in a job that involves hosting guest writers and tutors who regularly read aloud from their work. I've learned from many brilliant performances week after week. These are the main things I try to bear in mind at events of my own:

- It's not all about me. I try to forget how nervous I am by focusing on the audience. I remind myself of those essential messages and think about what others will want to hear rather than how I'm feeling about delivering the reading.

- Experience tells me that readers switch off when being read to for too long. I try and break up passages from the text with commentary, explanation and context. The best readers can to do this fluidly and without apparent effort but it comes with practice. Another benefit of this is that readers are more likely to connect with the human being who wrote the words, as well as with the words themselves.

- It goes without saying that it's best to practise reading aloud each extract before an event. I feel more confident venturing out in public if I've worked out all the nuances and inflections of a piece in advance.

- The best piece of advice I was given is this: don't rush to begin. Take time to establish your presence before you start

> speaking. This isn't egotistical but simply what the audience expects and has come for. In the end, remember, they're urging you to read well. They're on your side.

What Rachel says highlights the fact that we are all different, but that the main thing is to find what works best for us.

I hope that you have found these comments by writers helpful. They all have useful methods of developing their speech. Although they specialise in different fields of writing, they all say the same thing: read well, perform well, however you get there.

The key points for me as a performer are to know as much of my work by heart as possible and to remain emotionally connected to what I am saying. I sometimes allow myself to imagine that the audience is not there and I let my eyes hover over their heads so that I do not make eye contact with anyone for too long. Looking at a few people directly for just a couple of seconds keeps me connected to them. Any longer than that and I start to smile (when I shouldn't) or, even worse, stutter! This may not work for others. For instance, as noted above, Michelle Green likes to make regular eye contact with the audience. This does not work for me and it may not for you either. Often I find that it depends on the size of the audience and venue: smaller, more intimate settings such as libraries compel you to make eye contact. In larger outdoor events, where people are further away, it seems easier not to.

Getting your work out there

Be proactive and get involved in local groups; every town and city has workshop facilities to help writers to develop on the stage. Pubs, libraries, community centres and theatres are common places for performance. Set up your own performance group at university with some fellow students. Find out about the dates and venues for annual literature festivals: ring or email the organisers and ask them if you can read at one of their events. In the UK, the BBC is an excellent showcase for new writers. Getting a reading slot on a local radio arts show is not impossible. Email the show that you are interested in and send a sample of your work. That is how I began, and I am very glad I did this. It resulted in a series of short readings spanning over two years. If they like you, they will certainly remember you!

Websites are great to send your work to. In the UK, examples include Viral Verse and Rainy City Stories. Find out which websites publish work by writers local to you and email them. Visit your local library and bookshops, which are very helpful in holding events for students and other writers. *The writer's market* and *Writers' & artists' yearbook* are particularly useful guides for all. They include general and specific advice on getting your work out there.

Lastly, remember that as you become more involved in putting your work out there vocally, your voice will become stronger. One opportunity will lead to many more. All the writers who have contributed to this chapter are living proof of this: we all began somewhere. Find your true voice and *use* it.

Chapter Nine

The role of critical reflections and how to write them

Sharon Norris

During the course of your creative writing degree, it's likely you'll be asked to submit some form of critical reflection to accompany a creative writing portfolio. This could be a logbook, journal, commentary, oral presentation or a critical reflective essay. This chapter aims to help you understand what a critical reflection is, to familiarise you with the different forms of critical reflection you're likely to encounter and to enable you to feel more confident in approaching them.

Students sometimes struggle to understand why they're asked to write critical reflections and view them as less important than the portfolio. As a result, they often spend less time and effort on these than on other parts of the assessment. However, as the critical reflection element of any one module could account for as much as 30–40 per cent of the final mark, then whether you see its relevance or not, you neglect it at your peril!

It may help you to engage more with critical reflections once you know a bit about the rationale for setting them.

Why critical reflection?

BACKGROUND

Over the past twenty-five years, many practice-based arts and humanities subjects, from photography to dance, have been incorporated into the university syllabus. As with all practice-based subjects, including creative writing, you develop your skills over time and largely by 'doing'. The use of critical reflections as mode of assessment originates in the work of educationalists and researchers such as David Kolb, whose 'Experiential learning cycle' has been hugely influential (see Kolb, *Experiential learning*). Kolb sees the process of learning through 'doing' as an ongoing cycle, consisting of four stages:

1. concrete experience, where students gain hands-on experience of 'doing'
2. reflective observation, where they reflect on what and how they've learned while engaged in the process of doing
3. abstract conceptualisation, where each student formulates his or her own 'rules' to explain what they have learned
4. active experimentation, where, having formulated their 'rules', they then test these out.

The whole process starts all over again when learners find themselves in the next situation where they have to learn something new.

Other useful things about critical reflections

It's helpful to bear in mind that the rationale for setting critical reflections is to make you more aware not just of *what* you learn but also of *how* you as an individual learn.

125

However, there are other reasons why critical reflections are useful and a range of ways in which they can help you develop your writing skills.

They link you to a wider literary tradition

There's a strong tradition of critical reflective writing in English literature, that is, of individuals reflecting on why they became writers, why they chose to write in a particular way or how they came to develop a new genre of writing. Famous examples include Wordsworth and Coleridge's 'Preface' to *Lyrical ballads* and George Orwell's essay 'Why I write'. So, in writing critical reflections, in whichever form your institution requires, you're allying yourself with a long-standing literary tradition.

Adding another string to your bow

For many people, one of the main reasons for taking a degree in creative writing is to learn how to write in a range of styles and genres. Being open to learning how to write well across a variety of genres is important if you're serious about your craft as a writer, as the elements that determine what makes an effective piece of writing in one genre generally apply across the board. This also applies to critical reflections. More specifically, if you decide to specialise in non-fiction genres such as memoir or autobiography, learning how to reflect critically on your own motivations and approach to writing could prove invaluable. So try to view being asked to write critical reflections as the opportunity to add another string to your writing bow.

CREATIVE WRITING AS A REFLECTIVE/REFLEXIVE ACTIVITY

One final reason to embrace critical reflections, and perhaps the most important of all, is that the process of writing itself is fundamentally reflective. Writers are constantly reflecting: on the world around them, on their relationships and on their own inner thoughts. Celia Hunt and Fiona Sampson repeatedly make this point in *Writing: self and reflexivity*, though they also argue, drawing on the work of writing theorist Donna Qualley, that there's a difference between 'reflection' and 'reflexivity'. Reflection, they argue, happens mainly at an individual level (Hunt and Sampson, *Writing*, p. 4). However, Qualley suggests that *reflexivity* also involves engaging with 'another', including our self as 'other', and in so doing being open to change (Qualley, *Turns of thought*, p. 11).

What does it mean to be our self as 'other'? Many people, including Sigmund Freud, have talked about the creative process in general as involving a kind of 'doubling' of self. To understand how this relates to writing, think of the way in which novelists' own views, opinions and fantasies get translated into art via the process of making up characters. To that extent, many (perhaps all) novels are both fiction *and* autobiography and involve the writer being both subjectively involved in what they're writing about and one step removed from it.

At another level, as Spencer Jordan's chapter makes clear, the ability to be objective about (i.e. to stand back from) our own writing is crucial to the editing process. It's also crucial if we want to write effective critical reflections though in fact the ability to stand back from our writing is fundamental to what being a writer – any kind of writer – is all about. For that reason, it makes no sense to see critical reflections as something quite separate to your 'creative' writing.

Having examined the rationale for writing critical reflections, now let's think about how to approach writing them.

The different types of critical reflection

Students are often given very few guidelines as to how to go about writing critical reflections. In the case of critical reflective essays in particular (of which, more later), you're unlikely even to be given a question or essay title to work to. And, if students tend to spend less time on writing critical reflections, lecturers often have little time on a busy course timetable to factor in a lesson dedicated to the critical reflection. As a result, it can be hard to know where to begin if you're asked to write one.

A useful starting place can be to recognise that what you're being asked to do in a critical reflection is give an account of what you have done, and in particular what you have learned, in the process of producing either a single piece or an entire portfolio of writing. However, there are specific points you need to consider, depending on which type of critical reflection you're writing. The main types are:

- logbook
- journal
- oral presentation
- commentary
- critical reflective essay

Let's look at each of these in more detail.

Logbook

Some creative writing courses ask students to submit a logbook to accompany a particular piece or an entire portfolio of writing. A logbook is usually a fairly straightforward record of the work you did towards completing this. Logbooks are typically both less analytical and less formal than other types of critical reflection. Indeed, it's common for lecturers to tell students specifically *not* to edit their logs so they can get a better sense of the ongoing process.

You'll usually be given a word count for the finished log, and this should give you an idea of how detailed or otherwise you're expected to be. If you're asked to keep a logbook throughout the entire duration of a ten- or twelve-week module, the early weeks will probably contain less information, and the details you *do* log will usually cover points such as finding a topic or story idea and your initial background research. Later on, once you've started the process of drafting and editing the work your logbook accompanies, you'll have more to say.

It's important that you keep any logbook up to date, so you'll need to set time aside on a regular basis to add any new entries. Make sure you record every activity and the date and time you undertook it. This includes any planning you did towards something in the future. Your entries could be as simple as 'Got Mr Brown's phone number. Rang up and arranged to interview them next week', but you'll also need to make clear as you go along how anything you log links to your final piece. In the example above, you should already have noted somewhere in the log why 'Mr Brown' was worth interviewing and how he's relevant to what you're writing about, e.g., 'As my main character Tom is a fisherman, I hope to get more information from Mr Brown about the Whitby fishing fleet during the 1980s.'

JOURNAL

Journals are much the same as logbooks in that you're expected to update them on a regular basis (usually either daily or weekly). If you're asked to submit one, it's important that you follow any guidelines as to how often you're expected to update it. Journals too are usually submitted as an accompaniment to a creative piece, and, as with the logbook, the purpose of a journal is to allow you to record details of your progress towards completing this and to provide some context to it.

One important difference between a journal and a logbook is that, generally speaking, journals are written in more continuous prose whereas logbooks can simply be a series of extended notes and usually don't have to be written in proper sentences. Compare the two examples in the box below.

Sample logbook entry

Rang David Martin today. Managed to set up an interview for my feature – 3.40 Tuesday 16th at the Dove. Result!

Sample journal entry

Today I rang David Martin from the BBC to ask if I could do a background interview with him for my feature. He agreed, and we've arranged to meet up at the Dove on Tuesday 16th at 3.40 p.m. I am delighted as I've been trying to arrange this interview for the past two weeks.

On some creative writing degree courses, you may be asked to keep a more general daily journal or a diary that includes your thoughts on your writing and any ideas you have, especially in your first year. Many creative writing programmes also ask students (again especially in the first year) to keep a journal of free-writing, where you write the first thing that comes into your head. In both these cases, you wouldn't normally be asked to hand your journal in. If you were, either it wouldn't be marked, or any mark given would account for only a small percentage of your final mark. The main purpose would be to encourage you to get into the habit of writing regularly.

However, if you're asked to submit a journal of your progress towards completing a piece or portfolio of creative work as part of the assessment for a given module, this could account for a significant percentage of the overall grade.

Oral presentation

Although the focus of this chapter is written critical reflections, you could be asked to give an oral presentation on what you've learned on a particular module. A key difference between this and written forms of critical reflection is that *how* you presented would also be important. Also, if asked to give an oral presentation, you'd normally only be expected to reflect on part of the course, and, in general, presentations are less detailed than written critical reflections.

Commentary

Usually commentaries and critical reflective essays are both a bit more formal and more 'academic' than journals

131

or logbooks. This is especially true of critical reflective essays, which are discussed in more detail below. As with other written forms of critical reflection, you'll normally be given a word limit, so you should at least be able to work out how detailed you need to be. The length of commentaries varies from institution to institution (and from module to module within a given programme of study). It will also vary depending on which *year* of study you're in. For example, it's common for students in first and second year to be asked to write 500–1,000-word commentaries and for final-year students to be asked for commentaries that are anywhere between 1,000 and 2,000 words.

If you are asked to write a commentary, your assessment guidelines will probably say something like, 'Write a 500-word commentary to accompany your portfolio' then give little, if any, additional advice. Different institutions interpret the word 'commentary' in different ways, but usually you'll be expected to focus more on the creative work or 'end product' you submit than on the *process* of writing. As a result, you'll be expected to refer constantly to the finished creative piece in your commentary. Commentaries are generally also *retrospective*: in other words, they work backwards from the finished creative piece to discussing how it came to be written rather than the other way round (which would be more typical of the critical reflective essay).

CRITICAL REFLECTIVE ESSAY
The critical reflective essay is one of the most popular forms of critical reflection, though often the one that causes the

•

most grief. For this reason, the remainder of this chapter will focus on trying to demystify this strange, hybrid creature. We'll look at why it sometimes causes confusion and at how to write one.

Demystifying the critical reflective essay

Virtually everyone on a creative writing degree course will have written an academic essay at some point in their life, and critical reflective essays are like any other academic essay in so far as they have a beginning, middle and an end and the writer is expected to take a critically objective stance towards the topic (even if it is your own work). Also, as with other academic essays, you'll be expected to employ 'scholarly apparatus', in other words, to include footnotes and a bibliography and to follow the appropriate conventions for referencing and quotations.

However, there are some key differences between a critical reflective essay and what we might call a 'standard' academic essay. In order to be able to write effective critical reflective essays, it's useful to be aware of the ways in which they differ from the sort of academic essay you'll have written to date.

The main differences are as follows:

- Usually you're given no question.
- The focus is on your own work, not on someone else's.
- You are allowed to use the first person ('I', 'me', etc.).
- You are unlikely to have written, or even encountered, one until now.

Let's examine these four points in more detail.

Studying creative writing

No specific question
Up until now, you will have been used to essay questions that were quite specific, such as 'The origins of the Second World War may be found in the terms of the treaty of Versailles. Discuss', or 'How does Sylvia Plath use imagery in the poem "Daddy"?' However, if you're asked to write a critical reflective essay, the likelihood is you'll simply be told to: 'Write a critical reflective essay.' That said, you will get *some* guidance in so far as you'll be given a word limit, so, once again, as with the other forms of critical reflection discussed, you'll have some idea of how detailed you're expected to be. And, as noted above, you'll also be aware that it has to be written in the form of an academic essay, with all that entails.

THE FOCUS IS YOUR OWN WORK
The second big difference between critical reflective essays and 'standard' academic essays is that, unlike English literature essays, for example, the focus is not someone else's work but your own – in other words, something you'll have been intimately involved in creating. In some ways, that makes it easier as you'll know your 'topic' inside out, but this can also make it more difficult to be objective. This really is a situation where you have to be a 'doubled self' in order to be able to write critically and analytically about your own work.

USE OF THE FIRST PERSON
With most academic essays, you're not allowed to use the first person ('I') or to include any reference to yourself. However, if you were writing about your own work, and what (and how) you've learned that you've been able to

apply in your writing, it would sound odd and rather disingenuous if you were to write about these things in the third person. That would be a bit like me saying here about myself, 'Sharon Norris thinks that students don't spend enough time on their critical reflections.' However, in my experience, it's the fact that they're allowed to write in the first person in critical reflective essays that often confuses students the most and sometimes causes them to forget that they need to remain critically objective. Being allowed to use 'I' and being asked to focus on your own work shouldn't be taken as an excuse to 'splurge' about your relationship, your new coat or your social life – unless, of course, any of that is somehow relevant to how you came to write your portfolio. Even then, you'd have to make the connection very clear! Some students also think that because they're allowed to use the first person they can be more informal in the language they use. However, your writing style and vocabulary should be appropriately 'academic' throughout.

You're unlikely to have written one before

Most students, when asked to write their first critical reflective essay at university, won't ever have read one before, let alone written one. This means that you and the majority of your fellow students will have no previous experience to draw on. This difficulty is compounded by the fact that lecturers are often unclear about the rationale for setting them. And, as they are a relatively new form of essay, your lecturers are even less likely than you are to have been asked to write a critical reflective essay at school, or even at university.

Dealing with these difficulties

Here are some tips to help you tackle the difficulties listed above. As I go along, I'll be illustrating the points I make with examples taken from a particularly good undergraduate critical reflective essay written by one of my former students, Emma Thompson, where Emma was reflecting on her experience of writing a feature on homelessness for a non-fiction course.

Set yourself a question

In the absence of prompt questions from your tutor, an easy solution is to set your own. This could be something like 'What did I learn from this module?' or 'What would I do differently next time?' You should say in the introductory paragraphs what issue or question you're going to be addressing and then use this as a focal point around which to structure your thoughts in the remainder of your essay. Here's how Emma tackled this.

> This essay explores the decisions I made with regard to the form, subject and tone of my work and how I came to make them. I also discuss the position of the writer and the importance of imagination when writing non-fiction.

Make the central focus your creative work, and back up what you say

As the point of a critical reflective essay is to make you think about what and how you've learned in the process of planning, writing and editing a portfolio or single piece of writing, you really do need to focus on these things. As with any academic essay, you need to give evidence to back up what you say. Quoting directly from your work, and especially if you compare/contrast earlier versions of a given piece with the final version, can be a useful way of demonstrating both how your work improved over time with careful editing and of backing up any claim you make about how you were able to apply what you learned on the course to your own writing practice. Here's another example from Emma's essay which illustrates the point:

> After a lecture on the importance of linking one paragraph to the next I made several adjustments. For example, I changed 'Greg Hands MP is a member of the Communities and Local Government Committee which last month published a report called "Housing and the Credit Crunch" to 'A parliamentary select committee recently addressed the urgent need for government to go further in order to help these homeowners. Greg Hands MP is a member of the Communities and Local Government Committee which last month published a report called "Housing and the Credit Crunch".' The purpose of rewriting this link was to improve the transition from one paragraph to the next in order to present a more cohesive article, and I continued to edit other links between paragraphs.

If you want to quote at length from an earlier draft but are worried about going over the word limit, one way to get round this is to include the whole of the earlier draft(s) as an appendix at the back of your essay. As appendices aren't included in the final word count, you can simply refer the reader or marker to the appendix without having worry about using up your precious word allocation in long quotations.

'I am writing an academic essay'

As noted above, it's important not to see the critical reflective essay as a kind of 'confessional', where you tell everything about yourself. Yes, you *are* allowed to write in the first person and the focus *is* your own work, but you still need to be critically evaluative and objective in what you write; you need to be a 'doubled self'. Always remember, 'I am writing an academic essay.' You could even try repeating this to yourself as a kind of mantra while you're writing. That way you're already linking 'I' with 'academic essay' in the same sentence.

Remember too that as you *are* writing an academic essay, you'll need to use the usual scholarly apparatus, including a bibliography. The point of having a bibliography, even if you *are* writing about your own work, is that, as with any academic essay, you need to be able to put what you say within a wider context. Without wider reading and research, students often imagine that they're the only person who's ever written on a particular theme or the only writer ever to have used a particular technique. The following extract from Emma's essay underlines this.

> It was the quantity of research that I accumulated, however, that proved to be the greatest difficulty I experienced during the planning stage. I had chosen the broad subject of charities and their struggle to survive the credit crunch as my subject. The impact of the economic downturn on fundraising for charities had already been widely reported so I looked for a new angle.

Although Emma had undertaken so much background research and reading that she wasn't sure initially where to take her feature idea, it was reading round the topic that

Critical reflections

made her aware that (1) lots of other people had written on similar themes and (2) she needed to find a new angle. Here's a further extract from her essay which illustrates how reading (in this case one of the textbooks from the course reading list) also finally helped her to resolve the problem.

> In *Telling true stories: a non-fiction writers' guide*, a chapter on how to find a good topic to write about suggests, 'When a story has been heavily covered, reposition the camera. Pull in from the wide, news-gathering angle. Look for a close-up angle on the story that hasn't been told.' Following this advice, I focused on two angles that I felt had not been fully explored within this well-documented subject. The first was the emotional cost that homelessness has on families and the second was the link between the financial difficulties that charities are experiencing and the rise in demand for their services.

A key part of writing an academic essay – any type of academic essay – is an awareness of how others have tackled the same sorts of issues, whether it be other historians who've analysed the Treaty of Versailles or other writers who've struggled to work out 'what's the story?'

Find out what you need to know and ask to see sample essays

If you're given little extra information or even a question when asked to write a critical reflective essay, it's all the more important that you follow the guidelines you *are* given. It's just possible that you'll receive some additional instructions beyond 'Write a critical reflective essay' such as 'focusing on your choice of topics in the portfolio'.

139

If so, follow these to the letter – and if you're told to double-space or print on one side of the page only, that's what you need to do. Also, be sure to read any course handouts or books that cover the critical reflective essay (including this one!). Finally, don't be afraid to ask your lecturer if she or he can provide you with some sample critical reflective essays so you can see how it's done.

WRITING A CRITICAL REFLECTIVE ESSAY
Having looked at how to deal with some of the difficulties posed by critical reflective essays, now let's focus on how to go about writing them and what to include.

Make a plan
Once you've decided on the specific question or issues you intend to address, it's a good idea here (and with any longer commentary) to write out a short plan. This needn't be any longer than half a page of bullet points. It's easier to add or change the order of material at this stage than after you've started writing.

Choices
An important element of your essay should be a discussion of the choices you've made such as how you decided on your subject matter or topic, or your chosen form.

Putting theory into practice
What you mustn't do is simply regurgitate what you covered in class from week to week. The tutor knows this – and possibly even wrote the course. Concentrate on detailing how you've been able to put this into practice. Be explicit about this by citing examples from what you've written.

Dilemmas

You'll also need to discuss any dilemmas or difficulties you encountered, how you dealt with these, and, if relevant, why you decided to take one particular course of action rather than another to resolve them.

Back up what you say and use quotations that are relevant

Always give examples to back up any claim or assertion. Linked to this, make sure that any quotation from another source, such as a book or article you've read, is relevant to the specific point you're trying to make – and that you reference it properly.

Be critically evaluative

Don't be afraid to discuss what *didn't* work as well as what did. Remember, we often learn as much (sometimes more) from our mistakes as we do from our successes. And, as you'll be writing after you've completed your portfolio, it's important to reflect on whether things turned out as you'd expected or not – for example, whether your decision to experiment with a particular form or technique was successful.

Situate your work in a wider context

As noted above, you'll need to demonstrate that you are able to situate your work within a broader context. If you're submitting a portfolio of flash fiction on the topic of erotic obsession, for example, you'll want to refer to other flash-fiction writers who've covered similar themes (and to note how yours is different). You'll also want to refer to any relevant textbooks. In this way, you'll be demonstrating your knowledge of the wider area and your awareness of how your work fits into it.

Focus on what you've learned
Perhaps above all, the key thing is to focus on is what you've learned from the experience of planning, writing and editing creative work and the things you've learned that you'll be able to apply in the future. Here's one final extract from Emma's essay, taken from her conclusion, where she makes this explicit:

> The process of writing this topical feature has been a useful experience. In particular, I am now aware of the dangers of doing too much research and the difficulties that that entails. Useful techniques such as bullet-pointing specific sections in order to structure the story and thoughtful interviewing have helped me in the planning and writing stages, and I intend to use the skills I have learnt in future freelance writing.

Avoid over-personalising
Remember that any personal information has to be relevant to the topic.

Academic conventions
Don't forget to include a bibliography and to apply the appropriate conventions for footnotes and referencing. Make sure you know which system your creative writing programme uses (MLA, Harvard, etc.) and follow it.

Apply the usual rules
The rules of good writing apply to critical reflections too, so be sure to allow yourself time to redraft and edit. Be

clear, direct, concise and make sure you check your spelling, grammar, punctuation and layout.

Keep a log

One final tip: as you'll be writing about the process via which you came to complete your portfolio or single piece of writing, it's useful to keep a log of all the things you do from week to week, whether you're asked to or not. It's difficult to keep track otherwise, especially as you won't be writing your critical reflective essay until the final weeks of term.

Conclusion

Try not to see critical reflections as second-class citizens to your more 'creative' work. Aside from any other justification, the students I've taught have often talked about the sense of achievement they've gained from critical reflections and how, in the process of planning and writing them, they've realised just how much effort they've put into their work across the term.

If marks for the critical reflection are easy to lose because you don't know what's required or you don't allocate enough time for writing them, they're just as easy to gain once you *do* know and *do* take a bit more time over them.

Chapter Ten

Assessment: how it's done and its implications for your work

Helen Kidd

Creative writing is now well established as an academic subject. That means that the assessment process you encounter has been carefully considered, to provide you with ongoing structure in order to direct your learning and give you clear markers as to how you are developing. It will help you to think of it in this way and to view the grades and feedback you received as way-markers rather than as hurdles that have to be jumped.

This chapter aims to clarify how the assessment process works, what kind of direction assessment offers and how lecturers can provide you with crucial information about your strengths and your weaknesses, using assessment criteria, grades and further feedback to assist your development as a writer.

There are other ways of engaging with creative writing, such as writers' workshops and short (non-assessed) courses. A degree course differs particularly in this respect. It measures your progress using clearly defined criteria and gives you the opportunity to build on these.

Formative and summative assessment

Throughout your course you will experience two types of assessment: *formative* and *summative*. While formative assessment does not contribute directly to your grades, summative assessment does. Before we examine the assessment criteria in detail, it would be useful to tackle what each of these processes involves.

FORMATIVE ASSESSMENT

Formative assessment is essentially an *ongoing* dialogue with your tutors and fellow-students. You will engage in assignments, writing exercises, presentations and workshop discussions. The insight or guidance you receive on these is designed to give you a realistic ongoing appraisal of your work and the tools for self-appraisal. All of this is intended to lead up to *summative assessment* and to give you the best opportunity to present polished portfolios to clear deadlines. As you progress, so too will your learning curve. You will become more skilful at editing your own work and more confident in owning your own writing process.

The most common forms of formative assessment are as follows:

Logbooks

Some university creative writing programmes ask students to keep a regular logbook. Take care not to confuse these with notebooks or journals. A logbook is a brief summary of what you have covered each week. It provides ongoing evidence of your engagement with the course. Although logbooks are usually not assessed per se, your tutor may ask to see your log at different points during the term, so he or she can then give you feedback on where your focus needs to be strengthened. The logbook therefore contributes to your formative assessments. However, it also provides a useful reminder of your progress across the entire course and useful material for any critical reflection (see below).

Notebooks

Your tutor will normally encourage you to keep a notebook, if you don't already. These are for ideas, rough drafts and odd lines of dialogue, poetry or reflection. Occasionally your tutor might ask to see a page or two, to get an idea of how your initial ideas are developing.

Journals

You tutor may also recommend that you keep a diary or journal. These are entirely for your own benefit. Diaries are usually kept on a daily basis. With a journal, you can choose to write only when you have something particular you want to say. Both are discursive tools, in other words a place where you can reflect on things and talk to yourself about how you feel you are progressing. Both are usually private, although some students keep diaries/journals in the form of a blog in which they share their progress and ideas with their peers.

Workshopping

Workshops offer the opportunity to engage in evaluation of your fellow-students' work. However, as Jennifer Young's chapter on workshops stresses, the practice you get in discussing others' work will sharpen your ability to assess your own writing. Workshopping is at the core of ongoing formative assessment and provides a strong foundation and preparation for summative assessment.

Self-assessment
This is obviously related to workshopping, but your powers of self-assessment will also develop across the entire course as you grow more aware of the demands of your discipline and of your own learning process. Increasingly, you will be asked to feedback your own self-assessment in class and in tutorials, following which your peers and teachers will assess how realistic you are being, so this is an important part of your formative process.

Drafts
Make sure you keep a folder with all the drafts of any work in progress, especially if you prefer to edit on screen. This serves two purposes. First, you don't run the risk of losing material you might later want to recover. Second, your tutor may want to discuss the relative merits of different drafts and give you clear guidelines as to where your work succeeds and where it needs more focus. This kind of formative assessment is invaluable, as often you need an outside eye to give objective evaluation. You can also quote from earlier drafts in your critical reflection in order to demonstrate how your work has progressed over time.

SUMMATIVE ASSESSMENT
Assessment timetable
Some creative writing degree programmes set their summative assessments at the end of each term while others have 'staggered' assessments which means you'll be asked to submit certain parts of your assessed work earlier in the term, for example, at the end of Week 4 or Week 6. Also,

some degree courses are based entirely on continuous assessment while others include an exam component.

The different varieties of summative assessment
The grade for each individual course on your degree programme will be based on your performance across a range of summative exercises, though the number of pieces of work and the relative weighting given to each component varies from institution to institution. The component given the highest weighting (usually between 70–80 per cent of the total) will usually be a portfolio of your own creative work.

Portfolio
This is generally the central component of the summative assessment for any given course on a creative writing degree programme. Depending on the module, the focus may be on one particular piece of writing, for example a short story or feature, or on several different examples. Usually portfolios have a word limit of between 3,000 and 4,000 words, or less in the case of poetry modules.

The remaining percentage of your grade is likely to be based on your mark for one or more of the following types of summative assessment:

Critical reflection
This is the section of your submission where you spell out your method of working and what you have learned. The different forms of critical reflection are discussed in more detail in another chapter; however, you could be asked to write anything from a 500-word commentary

to a 2,000-word critical reflection essay. A critical reflection essay of this length would normally be worth around 20–30 per cent of the overall mark for a given module.

Essay
Depending on the area covered by a given module, you could be asked to write a standard academic essay on a topic such as the development of a particular form or genre of writing, e.g., the sonnet or the short story. Essays usually account for anything from 20 per cent to 50 per cent of the overall mark.

Presentation
On some creative writing courses, students are asked to give a presentation, either on their own or as part of a group (see also 'Group exercise', below). You may also be asked to give a presentation as part of your formative assessment. The length, topic and nature of this varies from institution to institution; however, typically the marks awarded for this account for between 10 per cent and 20 per cent of the overall mark.

Exam
Not all creative writing degree programmes have exams. Even if they do, not all modules within the degree programme will have them. For those that do, the exam could be anything from one to three hours long. The nature of creative writing exams varies. At some institutions, the exam focuses on particular aspects of writing history or writing theory, while at others students are required to write a piece of creative work under exam conditions. On modules that have exams as part of the summative

assessment, the mark for this usually accounts for between 30 per cent and 50 per cent of the overall grade.

Group exercise
Summative assessment sometimes includes a mark for your own individual contribution to a group exercise set by the tutor. You could be asked to write something collectively, or to visit a writing-related venue and write a report on it, or to research, write and deliver a presentation on a particular topic. Group exercises are often assessed earlier in the term for those courses that have staggered deadlines. Generally, you would be allocated a mark for your own individual contribution. Typically, any mark awarded for group work would be worth 10–20 per cent of the overall mark.

Engagement
On some courses a percentage of the overall mark may be awarded for the extent to which the tutor thinks you've engaged with the course. In some cases, this will simply be based on your performance in class. In others, your tutor might set a given task aimed at encouraging your engagement with writing as a whole. I am particularly keen on including a percentage grade for engagement at Level 6 on my poetry course. Students must organise, publicise and plan a public reading of their poetry. Typically, the engagement component of any course is worth somewhere between 10 per cent and 20 per cent of the overall mark.

Pitches and proposals
It's common for creative writing degrees to include a compulsory course on the business side of writing. This is usually

undertaken in the final year of the degree. The type of summative assessment for these courses varies from one institution to another. However, as these courses are designed to make you focus on the practicalities of getting your work published, the summative assessment here may include a pitch, synopsis or a book proposal, along the lines of what you'd be required to submit to a publisher or an agent. The relative weighting given for each of the assessment components in a course like this varies between institutions.

Dissertation
This is a project entirely of your own devising, but one which has to be designed with, agreed to and signed off by your tutor, who will ask you searching questions about research and time management. Usually you would work closely with a tutor, who is there to monitor and to offer ongoing formative advice and assessment. It differs from set courses in that you have to be at the helm constantly and provide regular updates to the tutor. It gives you the opportunity to become more of an independent learner and is invaluable for planning and creating synopses for your later career. The overall weighting of the dissertation varies.

Peer assessment
Finally, in addition to the informal advice you receive from your fellow students in class, some degree programmes (or individual courses within a programme) ask students to evaluate each other's performance as part of the *summative* assessment process. However, in this case it will comprise only a small percentage of the overall grade (usually no more than 5–10 per cent), and the tutor will monitor the process so that any bias can be compensated for if detected.

Other important points about summative assessments

Students with special requirements

If you have a disability or a medical condition that affects your ability to make the deadline or to complete an exam in the time given (for example, if you are visually impaired or have dyslexia), you will often be given extra time to complete assessments. However, it's important that you let your department know about this as soon as possible so they can make any necessary arrangements or agree any extension in advance, and, more generally, so they are aware that you may need extra support such as printed copies of lecture notes.

Feedback

When you get your work back after it has been marked, it will be accompanied by feedback sheets, which will explain to you in detail how the marker(s) have arrived at their evaluation and what you should take forward and develop as you continue your course. Always make sure you collect your work after it has been marked so you can use the feedback you have been given to improve your writing. If you're disappointed in your grade or if you don't understand the marker's comments, make an appointment to see your tutor so you can discuss these things.

The assessment process

Degree classifications

In the UK, for example, universities have a standard set of percentage marks and degree classifications, which are as follows:

- 70–100 per cent (First Class)
- 60–9 per cent (2:1)
- 50–9 per cent (2:2)
- 40–9 per cent (Third)
- 0–39 per cent (Fail)

From the second year of a three-year Bachelor of Arts degree course (Level 5) onwards, your grades for each module you take count towards your final degree classification. At most institutions, your marks at Level 5 will account for 40 per cent of your final degree grade and Level 6 (your final year) 60 per cent. But you need to check in your creative writing programme handbook to confirm this.

ASSESSMENT CRITERIA

Each creative writing degree programme has its own assessment criteria. It's important that you familiarise yourself with these. You should be able to find them in the programme handbook. If you come onto the course with all this information at your fingertips, you'll be able to plan and work accordingly.

The assessment criteria are *generic*, which means that although your tutors will be looking for particular things in the assessments you submit for each individual module, they give a general indication of the standard of work required in order to get a mark in a particular band in each course *and* overall in your final degree classification.

In order to receive an overall degree classification in any bracket, you would need to fulfil these criteria in your assessments for all or the majority of your courses in the final two years of your degree. Here are some sample assessment criteria:

70–100 per cent (First Class)

At this level, on the creative side, the work shows excellence in its originality and distinctive and appropriate sense of form, skilled application of techniques, clarity of expression, presentation in the appropriate format and a keen and appropriate sense of audience. On the critical side, excellent scholarly apparatus of referencing and bibliography, evidence of wide reading and strongly developed insights into the writing processes. The higher the mark at this top end, the more publishable the work will be.

60–9 per cent (2:1)

This work demonstrates a very good grasp of technical and stylistic demands appropriate to the genre, very good clarity of expression and some evidence of originality in the work. On the critical side, very good analysis and reflection, with a strong bibliography and scholarly apparatus.

50–9 per cent (2:2)

Evidence of ability to apply the techniques and stylistic demands of the chosen genre, with appropriate presentation and some originality, plus clarity of expression and linguistic competence. On the critical side, adequate analysis; basic scholarly apparatus of bibliography and referencing.

40–9 per cent (Third)

Some degree of ability and fair presentation, with the critical side containing some loose reflection, and a minimum scholarly apparatus.

> **0–39 per cent (Fail)**
>
> The work does not conform to the syllabus requirements and is not technically or critically competent.

Assessment criteria are often written in this sort of formal academic language.

If you are in any doubt as to what the assessment criteria for your particular degree mean, you should ask you tutor to explain. Some lecturers do this routinely as part of the course, but if they don't, or if they do and you're still confused, ask to see them for a one-to-one tutorial so you can go over any queries with them.

What do the examiners do?

Summative assessment is a rigorous process and never simply rests on the shoulders of one marker. In addition to the first marker, there is usually a second marker who second-marks a substantial sample of the work. At some institutions the second marker marks all of the scripts (this is called double-marking). The first and second marker both adhere to the assessment criteria, and, once they have finished marking, they meet together to discuss and compare their marks and comments and to agree the final grade.

Thereafter, a sample of the papers marked is sent to the external examiner. This is someone who works at another institution who can give a more objective view of the marking. All First Class papers are sent, and all Fails. Then at least one example from each band. If the markers have a wide discrepancy between their marks, these papers will also be sent, as will marks that fall on the borderlines between categories (i.e. 49 per cent, 59 per cent and 69 per cent) to ensure the work is definitely in the one band and not the other.

Usually exam boards are held at the beginning of each new term or semester to agree the marks from the term before. In the summer, the main exam board agrees students' grades for the whole year and, in the case of final year students, reviews their grades over the previous years and determines their final degree classification. The external examiners give their feedback on the process and standard of marking, and any problems are addressed. Finally, the degrees to be awarded are agreed by the entire panel.

So, as you can see, your marks are never simply the responsibility of one person alone but are carefully monitored and discussed throughout. Furthermore, not only are lecturers assessing you but they are also continually monitoring their own assessment procedures.

What are the markers looking for?

As the sample assessment criteria above indicate, you won't just be assessed on the ideas expressed in your writing, or on the subject matter, but on a range of additional elements. Although the wording of the assessment criteria will differ from one university to the next, they mostly cover the same areas in each degree banding.

Here are some of the key things the marker(s) will be looking for:

STRUCTURE

The marker(s) will be looking for *consistency* and *cohesion* in the structure of your work. This applies both to your creative work and to any essay or dissertation. In any fiction you submit you'll need to make sure there are no major inconsistencies in the time frame of what you've written and that that any plot hangs together properly.

You'll also need to think about the way the sequence of events unfolds in your piece and in what order. Again, this applies to fiction and non-fiction. If there are particular catalysts to the action, are these convincing (e.g., would receiving that letter really have affected character X in that way?).

The marker will also be looking at the ways in which you've dealt with any deeper themes, whether you've been able to sustain any key motifs and how have you woven these into the narrative.

CHARACTERISATION

The marker will be looking to see if you've taken time to build up a picture of your characters for the reader and have given sufficient detail to allow the reader to understand the way they think. They'll also consider how much backstory you've given and how well you've controlled the flow of information here.

STYLE

When it comes to the creative piece, this is all-important. You will need to demonstrate style and techniques appropriate to the genre and subject chosen. An obvious, if rather frivolous, example of inappropriate style would be a funeral lament or elegy written as a series of limericks. Another might be a confusing use of mixed metaphor or fiction for pre-teens written in long complicated sentences.

Style can also cover a number of narrative choices, including tenses (which need to be consistent) and narrative voice. It also has a bearing on a later point, the sense of audience/readership.

POETRY

There are particular things the marker will be looking for in any poetry submission. These include:

- how well you've been able to work within a genre where economy of language is key
- originality in your use of imagery
- awareness of the sound elements of language (i.e. in your use of onomatopoeia; alliteration, assonance, etc.)
- linguistic 'daring', such as neologisms (where you create new words) and ambiguity
- use of 'white space' and layout on the page
- syntax and lineation (including features such as run-on/enjambment).

You will likely be penalised for 'poeticalisms' such as archaic language, forced rhyme (where you choose a word that's inappropriate simply because it rhymes, or alternatively 'make' a word rhyme which doesn't usually) and forced metre (where you alter the way things would normally be said or written in order to fit the metrical format you've used).

LANGUAGE

The assessment criteria for your course may contain phrases such as 'uses appropriate diction, register and address'. This means that the language you use should be appropriate to the context. The marker will also be looking to see how well you've used any dialogue and whether you've used direct, free indirect or indirect speech. You'll also need to demonstrate a more general facility with things like being able to vary the length of sentences.

At a more basic level, the marker will also be looking at how fresh, as well as how appropriate, your vocabulary is, and how sensitive you are to the shadings and nuances of language. At all times, try to use fresh language and avoid clichés.

Awareness of your readership and audience

Writing is a generous act that involves the receiver as much as it does you. So it's not a case of swaggering but of finding out what suits the subject and the audience. The marker will want to see evidence of an appropriate awareness of your audience and, specifically, of your ability to gear your work to your intended readership. Is your feature on handbags the sort of topic *Men's Health* would cover?

'Scholarly apparatus'

With regard to dissertations, essays and critical reflections you'll be marked on your use of what's often called 'scholarly apparatus'. This refers to your ability to cite sources properly in any bibliography and to reference them correctly in the essay/dissertation itself according to whichever system your creative writing programme uses (e.g., Harvard).

Engagement with writing as a process

Another phrase you might see in the assessment criteria is 'shows evidence of engagement with writing as a process'. It should be obvious that you've worked hard at crafting, redrafting and editing your work. Creative writing is one subject where it's simply not possible to leave everything until the night, or even the week, before.

Imaginative input

This is perhaps the most contentious area because it is here that a piece of work can move from a competent, well-presented, technically polished piece to something striking, original and innovative. This is the area we cannot teach, only encourage, for example, through the use of exercises in class aimed at stimulating creativity and imagination.

Some basic points

You should also keep in mind the following basic but fundamental points as a way to avoid throwing away easy marks in your summative assessments.

Answer the question!

It may sound obvious, but one of the key things marker(s) look for is evidence that you have done what you were asked to do. In the case of an exam question or an essay, it's simple: make sure you answer the specific question you've been set and address the topic. If you're asked to write a critical reflective essay, you're unlikely to be given a question as such. However, you can set your own in order to focus your thoughts (see Sharon Norris's chapter on critical reflections for further details).

It's a bit less straightforward with the portfolio, where you're usually asked simply to 'submit a portfolio of creative work'. Once again, though, make sure you follow any guidelines covering the number of pieces you're expected to submit, or the genre, and any 'rules' or constraints such as 'at least one piece should be a short story'.

Word limit
Always make sure you adhere to the word limit. Most universities will allow you to go over or under this by up to 10 per cent, but no more, though you should confirm what the 'rules' are on your own programme.

Deadlines
You must keep to any deadline. You will normally be given these at the start of every term. It's important to find out as soon as possible when your deadlines are and to pace yourself accordingly. And if you're given a particular date and time for the course exam, make sure you turn up (and at the right location)! If you're ill and unable to submit your work or to attend an exam, you should inform your tutor or programme administrator as soon as possible. You'll probably be expected to fill out a form explaining why you failed to submit work or to attend the exam, and you may be asked to get a letter from your doctor confirming that you were unwell that day.

Bibliography
If you're asked to include a bibliography with an essay, dissertation or critical reflection, make sure you do so.

Turnitin and online submissions
Many universities ask students to submit online copies of their work to Turnitin or similar programs. These detect

if students have tried to submit work from another source as their own (e.g., an essay they found on the Internet). Often students are given the same deadline for submitting both the hard copy and the Turnitin versions of their work, but some institutions allow students extra time to submit the latter. It's important to find out when the deadlines are for each, as many institutions will give you a '0' for 'incomplete submission' if you submit the one version without the other.

As far as plagiarism is concerned, don't take the risk! Passing off someone else's work as your own is cheating, and you could end up being expelled from university.

Increasing numbers of institutions are moving to online-only submissions for summative (and sometimes formative) assessments. On the plus side, this means you can submit your portfolio at 3 a.m. if that's the only time you have, and you don't physically have to come into university to deliver your work. However, computers and computer programs can and do break down and invariably choose to do so just as you are about to press 'send' with three minutes to go before a deadline. If your institution operates an 'online-only' system for assessed work, or even if you're only required to submit an online *copy*, it's vital that you find out how the process of online submission works as soon as possible.

Layout and spacing
If your course has specific requirements about the layout of text, poetry being one particular example, then make sure you follow the rules. Most creative writing programmes ask students to use a 12-point font and double-spacing and single-sided printing when submitting work. Some

also ask for a wide margin or indented paragraphs. This is for your benefit really, as it enables the marker to write comments on your work, so failure to follow these guidelines could potentially limit the amount of valuable feedback you receive.

Spelling and grammar
You'll be expected to check your work in advance for any spelling and grammatical errors. These days, there's no excuse for not doing a simple spelling and grammar check on your computer, though you shouldn't simply rely on this, as spell-check facilities in word-processing programs aren't always accurate. Failure to do a spelling and grammar check suggests that you haven't bothered to edit your work.

Always read over your work before you submit
Finally, always give yourself time for one last read-through before submitting work for assessment. This allows you to pick up on any typos, omissions or non-sequiturs. If what you've written doesn't make sense to you, the chances are it won't make sense to the marker either!

USING FEEDBACK
You will receive feedback on both formative and summative assessments continuously throughout your degree course. In the *formative* context, as noted, this could include feedback from your fellow students, for example within a writing workshop. You can also expect to receive feedback from your tutor. This could be either written, for example, any comments she or he makes on your logbook,

or oral, in the form of any feedback you receive in class or in one-to-one tutorials.

How to use assessment to take you forward

Here are some final points for you to bear in mind:

- Familiarise yourself with the assessment criteria and what they mean to further your work and build on your existing achievements.
- Keep in mind the importance of using (different forms of) feedback, formative and summative, to improve your work.
- See assessment not as a trial but as a way to move forward with your writing and to receive yet more suggestions and input from your academic mentors.

A good style guide will prove invaluable and help you refine and retune those areas of your work where you might otherwise stumble.

In conclusion, your own insights and self-evaluation should develop throughout the course, so that you can take ownership of and monitor your development. Consequently, assessment should make sense to you and give you a solid foundation upon which to build. Obviously your future development as a writer will benefit from all the varieties of assessment on the course. Good luck on your creative path.

Chapter Eleven

What happens next? How to proceed after graduation

Sally O'Reilly

Preparing the ground: what to do while you are studying

One of the great joys of being a student on a creative writing programme is that there are no limits on your imagination. You can experiment with form and genre and develop the craft and the art of writing until you begin to discover your own voice. Both your tutors and your fellow students can help this process, and their feedback and suggestions are essential to your learning. Above all, a well-structured creative writing programme offers a context for writing and the development of new work, which is not dependent on the vicissitudes or commercial demands of the publishing industry.

However, this doesn't mean that you can ignore such demands or treat your writing course as a comfort blanket, clinging to it for reassurance rather than taking account of the world outside. While it would be a mistake to obsess about your future career while you are studying, at the expense of developing your imagination and skill, it would be equally misguided to postpone all thoughts of life after your degree until the day after graduation.

From the very beginning, you should be thinking about your writing portfolio and developing your credibility as a writer. These are parlous times in the mainstream publishing industry – of which more later – but there are still opportunities there. You need to be focused and organised, perhaps compiling a list of relevant competitions, literary magazine and arts festivals as well as online writing magazines and communities. It is wise to make the most your tutors' contacts – and check out their noticeboards, both actual and virtual, for information about publishing opportunities and competitions.

In addition, try to become as well informed as you can about the publishing industry and the various imprints and houses (both global and independent) and literary agents. Don't be daunted by this. Although it sometimes seems as if agents and editors are interested only in writers who are famous already, they need people like you. The publishing industry also sees creative writing degree programmes as useful when seeking fresh talent. Publishers are actively seeking new voices, and one of those voices could be yours. This is where all your hard work and brilliant, original writing will come into its own.

Networking: actual and virtual

Talent is important, but it's unlikely that you will be 'discovered' on the basis of talent alone. If you read the biographies of any established author from any period in history you are likely to find that they became part of a writing community or network of some kind; that they were employed in a relevant field such as journalism beforehand; and that they worked in collaboration with understanding agents and/or publishers. This is true of Charles Dickens and George Eliot, and it's true of contemporary authors such as Nick Hornby and Zadie Smith.

The idea of the lone genius penning their masterwork in a garret is a compelling one, but it's not the way it works. (Not usually, anyway. All statements about writing careers come with the caveat: 'except for the exceptions'.) It is certainly important to write a great book, but it is also vital to make sure that you are giving yourself the best chance of getting it published by establishing a good network, which includes fellow writers – published and otherwise – events organisers, tutors, agents and even publishers.

Networking often gets a bad press. The assumption is that you have to be pushy and extrovert to do this successfully. The fact that 'who you know' is important is seen as an indication that publishing is run by cliques. But this doesn't mean there is a conspiracy to keep people out; what it means is that there are so many 'wannabe' writers out there that agents and publishers use whatever sifting process they can to limit the number of submissions they have to read. If they have met you, and talked to you, they are more likely to read your synopsis. Equally, if you have done your research and have found out about the kind of work they are interested in, you are more likely to send your work to the right person.

Therefore, it's important to follow up any contacts that your tutors set up with industry insiders: these links are vital. And it's also useful to stay in touch with all your student friends – they will be a useful source of information in the future, as well as potential readers of your work and a source of support if you feel ground down by rejection letters.

You might like to formalise this relationship with those you get on well with and organise regular meetings, perhaps a writing workshop or a Facebook page (see the section below for more information on social media and publishing). If you don't form a writing group with fellow students, seek out an established group in your area or set one up yourself. Your public library may run a group, or there may be information in local bookshops. UK-based students can contact the National Association of Writers' Groups for more information.

Writing conferences and festivals are also useful places to make new contacts and to keep up with new events. There is no need to attend the whole conference; instead, you can look at their programmes online to find out whether writers who interest you are speaking and whether any of the fringe events are relevant to you. UK festivals such as Edinburgh and Hay often have a mix of free and paid-for events; if money is tight, check out the free ones. There may be one-off workshops about different aspects of genre or publishing, and both the speakers and the other participants may be potential contacts. It is a good idea to approach speakers to ask follow-up questions and to talk about their work, particularly if they are writing in the same field as you. You could also give your contact details to fellow writers and follow up any contact with an email as soon as possible afterwards. However, it is not a good idea to take your unpublished manuscript to these events and ask people to read it: you will just seem like a desperate amateur.

The most effective approach is to make conversation, to get to know people, and to try to be a useful contact yourself. For instance, if you know of a writing competition that's coming up or a new publishing initiative, talk to people about it rather than keeping the knowledge to yourself. Effective networking is about sharing and co-operating, so the more you can offer to your new contacts the more they are likely to want to establish a link with you.

The myth of raw talent

Confidence is a useful attribute for an author. Self-doubt can be incapacitating and can affect both your writing output and your ability to withstand the inevitable rejections and disappointments that come your way. But being arrogant about your talent and assuming that you are so good that you will be 'discovered' is misguided. Currently, there are more than 70 higher education institutions in the UK alone offering degrees or further degrees in creative writing, and every year hundreds of their creative writing graduates flood onto the writing scene. (One hesitates to say 'job market' as there are so few jobs to be had.)

Apart from that, there are innumerable writers of all ages who are anxious to find a public outlet for their work, whether they are novelists, poets, dramatists or even would-be journalists. Therefore, if you want your writing to be read, you will need to network and to keep up to date with what is happening both locally and nationally. You may be right: you may be the most talented writer on your course or in your workshop group. And this may be the factor that ultimately makes you a success. But it won't happen if you don't make that talent conspicuous to other people. You need their attention, and you need to establish a place in existing writing networks. I write this although I know that writers are, almost without exception, rugged individualists rather than jolly team players. You may have to force yourself to attend a networking event or launch party. But force yourself you must.

The reassuring news for the shy or introverted writer is that not all networking has to be face to face these days. Social media such as Facebook and Twitter offer an opportunity to form links and alliances with writers and writing-industry professionals online. Start by setting up a Facebook page or expanding what you already have. You may want to start a separate writing page if your current page is full of photos of you getting drunk on holiday and cavorting with your friends. Using social media professionally means promoting a certain aspect of yourself rather than letting it all hang out.

Once you are networked in this way, you will automatically see regular updates about competitions, open mic events, new anthologies, book launches and so on, as well as hearing the opinions of famous writers at first hand. (Be wary: like the rest of the nation, they also post random musings about the latest TV drama and pictures of their cats.) Twitter works in a similar way, though for some reason it's more difficult to get well-known writers to follow you back. But you can use it to keep abreast of new developments, to follow agents and publishers and to get free writing tips and advice.

A warning. In fact, two warnings. First, don't rely exclusively on virtual networking. There is no substitute for getting to know actual people, in reality. So much of our human communication relies on non-verbal cues, and we learn so much from the physical presence of other people. Second, don't let the online aspect of your writing life loom too large. Writing itself must be at the core of everything you do if you are going to make the most of life after your degree, and social media has taken over as one of the prime suspects when it comes to destroying concentration and stealing time.

That said, it is certainly possible to promote your work online both by setting up your own website or blog (a blog is a micro website) and by posting your work onto existing sites. A blog is an online journal and a great space to share news, general writing tips and, perhaps, to post examples of your own work. There are also online writing magazines that operate in a similar way to traditional magazines: you submit your work and the editors will choose the pieces they think are the best or most suitable for their publication.

Getting published online

At the time of writing, one of the news items of the day was that, after 244 years, the *Encyclopaedia Britannica* would no longer be published in book format and would only be available online. While we might regret this, there is no escape from the fact that publishing is in the throes of revolutionary change.

As a writer at an early stage in your career, you will be wise to spread your net as wide as you can and be prepared to write in a number of different genres and within a range of formats. The Internet potentially offers you access to a huge number of readers. In early 2012, the website *Internet world stats* reported that 2,405,518,376 people across the world were using the Internet. Although the scale is daunting, and it can be hard to know how to begin or whether anyone in that great sea of people will be interested in what you have to say, it makes no sense to write only for the traditional, paper-based media, whether you are writing journalism, creative non-fiction, short stories, poetry or novels.

So the key question is: how do you get started? How do you find the outlet that is right for you and for your particular style or genre of writing? The first step is to go online as a reader and fan and to see who is out there and what they are doing. Develop your Facebook page and Twitter account so that you are in touch with as many established writers, publishers and agents as possible. You can also search the Internet using Google or another search engine to see what comes up under 'online writing' and other related headings. Again, the aim is to get as much information as possible. Don't be put off if there seems to be too much to take on board. Once you have seen what the options are, you can narrow your focus down to a small number of likely outlets for your work.

Another approach is to showcase your work by setting up your own blog. This is easy to do using platforms such as Wordpress or Blogger. A blog gives you the chance to write in more depth about your passions and opinions, though less is always more when writing online. Remember that attention spans are short and that people tend to browse when they are online rather than spending long periods of time reading one piece.

In addition to keeping your posts relatively short (I would suggest no more than 500 words), you should also see your blog as a communication tool rather than just a shop window or soapbox. The platform you use will offer you suggestions about how to do this using labels and words that are picked up by search engines, but it is also advisable to link your blog to your social-media sites and to share your new posts with your online contacts. A search engine will search the Internet looking for key words or phrases and compile an index of the information it finds. Internet users can then look for this information. It follows that if you use words that search engines are looking for, they will be picked up. Thus, if you blog about publishing news, key trends in publishing or famous authors, search engines will store this information.

The more frequently you blog, the more followers you will have, and, ideally, you should try and post at least once a week. Do bear in mind that this can be a distraction, just like all other forms of online writing, and limit yourself to blogging at certain times each week. And don't become addicted to your 'stats' page if you can possibly manage it; it really doesn't matter how many people in Alaska are reading your post at 3 a.m., though it is rather nice to know they are out there.

Online communities: dos and don'ts

The key to being a good citizen of the Internet is to share information and to act as a conduit, passing on tips and useful updates about competitions, new magazines, bursaries, interesting sites and so on. Writers who constantly use Facebook and Twitter to blast their friends and followers with information about their work come across as relentlessly self-serving – not to mention dull. Earn the right to let people know about your book launch or pub reading by telling people about other book launches and poetry readings first.

Most authors will now have a website or blog of some kind, and some of these are both lively and informative. Just as reading books helps your writing voice in general, you will only get the particular 'register' of online writing if you read widely and become familiar with the tone and style of writing in this way.

A word on ethics and the law. The Internet may be a 'virtual' place, but in legal terms it is real. The law is that if something is published online, it has the same status as a published document. If you are abusive or make offensive or insulting remarks to another person, this may therefore constitute libel. Of course, Facebook, Twitter and the Internet generally are full of people squabbling and making personal remarks. But I would advise against this. Not only is being offensive online potentially illegal, it is also unethical. My own tactic is to be scrupulously polite when using social media. If you do want to criticise someone, it is wise to examine your motives. Do you need to put your views across so vehemently? Might your comments harm someone else's reputation? The publishing world is small and cliquey, and the best advice I have ever had from a seasoned writer is to 'play nice'. Restrict yourself to posting comments you would say to someone in person and you won't go far wrong. Better still, I would suggest posting comments that you would not find hurtful if someone said them about you.

Whatever sort of writing interests you, there will be communities of writers out there who you can join. Equally, the Internet is spawning new ways of writing and new opportunities. One of these is National Novel Writing Month (NaNoWriMo). This is an annual writing event, which runs every November. Would-be novelists can sign up to write a 50,000-word novel in one month. As a participant you post your progress on the NaNoWriMo site (www.nanowrimo.org) and also join actual communities of writers in your local area.

Making the most of the local scene

The Internet is a great tool, but it's still vital to find out about what is going on in your local area. Find out about pub readings, literary activities in your library, any literary events or talks that are going on, and even literary festivals, which are becoming increasingly popular.

If there is no writing group in your locality, or you don't feel at home in the groups that do exist, then set up your own. You can advertise this in the local paper, ask writing friends you already know and just build gradually from there. A writing circle can be small: four people are enough, if they are committed and show up for each meeting. To make a group like this work, you should be certain that you are prepared to read the work of the other members as well as getting feedback about your own writing and be sure to pay careful attention to the work you read and give a measured, thoughtful opinion. Writers are sensitive, and the best writing groups are those in which members trust each other but are prepared to offer serious, constructive feedback.

Finding an agent and publisher

There are many routes to publication and to finding readers. But the traditional route is via an agent. This is still in some ways the simplest option, especially if you are writing fiction, but it is also one of the most challenging aspects of a writing career, because there are so many would-be writers chasing publishing deals, and most publishers won't look at a manuscript unless it has come via personal recommendation or an agent.

To find an agent, you must be well organised, diligent and persistent. Don't get too emotional about it: agents are business people who will take on clients if they think they are commercially viable. Some agents – and editors – talk about what they do in terms of 'love' and 'passion', which can be misleading. They do need to believe in your work and in your talent. However, it's not a personality contest, or a beauty pageant, and the more dispassionate and realistic you can be about finding both an agent and a publisher the better for your mental health.

Your starting point should be the *Writers' & artists' yearbook* (in the UK) or *Writer's market* (in America) which is published annually, in book format. It is still the definitive list of agents, publishers and writing professionals, and it is also packed with good advice. Work through this systematically, though not necessarily alphabetically. Start with the big agencies first: they like new voices, so you could be lucky. Go for newer, younger agents who are still building a list. As well as using the *Yearbook*, you will also need to research the market in terms of your style and genre of writing. Do some online research and see who represents your favourite authors and those who have influenced your work.

Check out each agent's website, find as much as you can about them. How do they like to be approached? How much of your work do they want to see? What kind of writers do they represent? How well known are their existing clients? Don't use gimmicks like fancy paper or wacky messages – agents dislike this.

You will need to go through much the same process when approaching a publisher. You can still contact the smaller presses direct: UK examples include Canongate, Tindal Street, Alma Books and Myriad Editions.

Self-publishing: the pros and cons

It is also worth considering going it alone and publishing your own work. It is now easier and cheaper to do this than it has ever been. Self-publishing using the Internet is very different from traditional vanity publishing, which involves paying a company to print a certain number of books, usually for a large fee. But sites like Lulu and Amazon's CreateSpace enable would-be authors to produce print editions of their books without going to a private publisher.

There is no need to stockpile large quantities of your books – print on demand means exactly that: your book is only printed when someone wants to buy it. As a self-published author, you can charge what you like, or even supply your books free, although some experts warn that cheap e-books are undermining the whole concept of paying a fair price for a book.

One of the great success stories in this field is Amanda Hocking, who has now signed a deal reported to be worth more than $2 million with US publisher St Martin's Press for her paranormal romance books. Hocking has also sold more than 1 million e-books herself for between $0.99 and $2.99. Amazon has been quick to see the advantages of e-publishing and publishes e-books for free, simply charging 30 per cent on the sale price for books published on Kindle.

The key problem for self-published writers is that there are so many books being produced, and it's extremely difficult to get publicity and profile for a self-published work. In an article that appeared in *Publishers' Weekly* in April 2010, Jim Milliot reported that 764,448 titles were produced in the USA in 2009 by self-publishers and micro-niche publishers, while a survey conducted by Bowker Market Research (UK) and published in *The Bookseller* in March 2012 found that e-books accounted for 5 per cent of consumer book purchases by volume by the fourth quarter of 2011, putting the UK 12–15 months behind the USA in terms of e-book market share. Purchases from e-book publishers are having a significant impact. Bowker estimated that 'perhaps a fifth' of total e-book purchases were made from self-publishers.

Staying motivated

If you are serious about your writing career, then you will have to be prepared to deal with rejection and disappointment and determined to keep writing even when you are feeling demotivated. The idea of an instant career has been disseminated by TV shows such as *The X Factor*. But in any field artists need to learn their craft and to continue to develop their skill and expertise, no matter what reaction they are getting from the professionals who can provide access to an audience – and sometimes even from that audience itself.

It can be hard to keep going if you feel isolated and irrelevant. Joining a writing workshop can help with this. As I have suggested, your fellow students can be useful in this respect. A weekly meeting with other writers can make the difference between writing and not writing, or, in other words, between being a writer and not being one.

Day jobs

Most successful writers have been very busy people, and many of them have had a day job. Great work has been produced under intense pressure: most of the classic writers who dominate English-literature syllabuses were involved in many other things apart from producing their Art. William Shakespeare, Jane Austen, John Keats, Charles Dickens and George Eliot all come into this category. George Orwell worked as a military policeman, schoolteacher, bookshop assistant, journalist, smallholder and post-office manager, as well as fighting in the Spanish Civil War. As if that wasn't enough, he was also a single parent. So if you need a day job, you'll be in good company.

The best day jobs are those which are (relatively) easy to run alongside your writing. Ideally, a good day job will offer you a degree of financial security so that you can focus on your artistic output. If you have a romantic idea about waiting tables while you write the modern *War and peace*, then be prepared to be dog-tired and pretty demoralised.

Ideally, try to find something that relates to your writing. Classic writer-friendly jobs include lecturing, publishing and journalism. A creative writing degree is a good way into any of these occupations, though personally I would advise a few years in the 'real world' between taking an undergraduate degree and embarking on the higher-degree programmes necessary to work in a university.

Publishing and journalism are popular careers, and competition for entry-level jobs is tough, but if you can get onto the first rung of the ladder, both career routes can aid your writing. Publishing will give you an insider view of a fast-changing market, and vital contacts. And both agents and publishers are happy to work with journalists because they are good with words – and willing to make revisions to their work without getting too upset.

But every writer is different, and you may find that for you working in a hat shop is the perfect balance with writing. A creative writing degree is also a useful degree for most generic graduate jobs. For example, according to a recent article in *HR Magazine*, accountancy firm Ernst & Young looks for skills in relationship development and problem-solving in graduate trainees, as well as determination and resilience and the ability 'to work hard and thrive in difficult situations'. In particular, the skills acquired when giving and receiving peer review for drafts in progress are highly transferable: ideally, you will have learned to focus on the opinions and creative output of your peers, understand different points of view, share ideas constructively and communicate sensitive information in a positive and constructive way.

Being a writer: the future starts now

So where does this leave you as you approach the end of this chapter and this book? Remember, there are many kinds of writers, and innumerable career paths. Not all writers are novelists or poets. You might put your skills to good use writing press releases for an organisation you believe in, or brilliant speeches or plain-English versions of complex, jargon-ridden documents. You might work as an online journalist, or as a researcher or copy-editor. One career can lead to another, or blur into another: journalists become ghost-writers; publishers become poets; speech writers become novelists. And many writers, if not most, run more than one career at a time and earn money in different ways, doing different things. The key to success is to find a way of living and earning that suits your character and your needs, artistic and practical. If your dream is to get that three-book deal, then this is likely to take time, and you will need to take the long view.

A congenial and flexible day job will help, as will determination and single-mindedness. A writer is someone who writes, regularly and with commitment. This writing may or may not be a source of income, and the key to happiness is to find a way to free yourself mentally and emotionally to the extent that your work doesn't stop you from committing your thoughts to paper. The friends and contacts you have made during your time at university will be just as important to you as the skills you have developed. Or it may be that your ambitions are realised in unexpected ways, by working in a field that is allied to writing but one that does not require you to write full-time. You may start up a publishing imprint, find work as an agent or realise that your vocation is actually teaching and helping the next generation to find the right words. Whichever route you take, your attitude to your creative writing degree is all-important, and, with a positive, forward-looking attitude, you may be surprised how many doors are open to you.

About the contributors

Ally Chisholm
Ally Chisholm has an undergraduate degree in writing, publishing and literature from Middlesex University, London. He took an MA in creative writing at Brunel University, specialising in the novel. He is currently studying for a PhD in literature at the University of Reading.

Lorna Fergusson
Lorna Fergusson is a novelist, short story writer and teacher. She runs Fictionfire, offering writing workshops and editing, critiquing and mentoring services. She has taught at Winchester University's writers' conference for twelve years and, over the past decade, on Oxford University's undergraduate diploma in creative writing, part-time and summer-school programmes.

Nabila Jameel
Nabila Jameel is a British Pakistani poet, working and living in Manchester. Her poems have been published in *Stand* magazine, the *Poetry review* and in *Out of bounds*, a recent anthology by Bloodaxe. She taught English in the further-education sector and now works for Hachette Books. She is working on her first poetry collection, which is a series of critical snapshots of society.

Spencer Jordan
Spencer Jordan is a writer and lecturer. He trained as a historian and completed his PhD at the University of the West

of England, Bristol, in 1999. He has a long-standing interest in creative writing, and his first novel was published by Macmillan in 2005. Since 2009 he has been Programme Director for postgraduate humanities degrees at Cardiff Metropolitan University.

Helen Kidd
Helen Kidd teaches English studies and creative writing at Ruskin College, Oxford. She is working on her fifth collection of poetry. She has collaborated with artists and musicians and on projects in prisons and schools. She was co-editor of the *Virago book of love poetry*, and her third collection, *Blue weather*, won the Cork Manuscript Award. In the 1990s she founded the cross-arts performance group Folding Air.

Sharon Norris
Sharon Norris is a writer, editor and musician. She trained as a journalist and has taught journalism and non-fiction at several UK universities. Most recently she was Senior Lecturer in Creative Writing at the University of Roehampton in London. She returned to university as a student in 2012, to study music production. She also contributed to another book in this series, *Teaching creative writing*.

Sally O'Reilly
Sally O'Reilly is the author of two novels published by Penguin and a career guide for writers (Piatkus). Her short stories have appeared in the UK, Australia and South Africa. She has taught creative writing at the Open University, the University of Portsmouth and Brunel University, where she is also completing her PhD.

Elizabeth Reeder
Elizabeth Reeder is a novelist and essayist. She teaches on the creative writing programme at University of Glasgow, convening the MLitt in creative writing, both the campus-based and online courses. She completed a PhD in English literature by submitting a novel as well as a creative/critical crossover element. Her novel, *Ramshackle* (Freight), was shortlisted for the Saltire award in 2012, and her second novel, *Fremont* (Kohl), was published in October 2012.

Shawn Shiflett
Shawn Shiflett is an associate professor in the fiction-writing department at Columbia College, Chicago. His novel, *Hidden place* (Akashic Books) was included in the *Library Journal*'s 'Summer Highs, Fall Firsts', a 2004 list of 'the most successful debuts'. He is currently finishing his novel, *Hey, liberal,* the story of a white boy at a predominately African-American high school in the late 1960s.

Jennifer Young
Jennifer Young is a senior lecturer in creative writing and an associate dean in the School of Humanities at the University of Hertfordshire. She completed her PhD in creative writing at the University of Southampton. Her writing includes magical realism, dystopian and historical fiction.

Bibliography

Useful websites

CreateSpace
www.createspace.com

Evernote
www.evernote.com

Julia Cameron's techniques
www.theartistsway.com

Kolb's 'Experiential learning'
www.learningandteaching.info/learning/experience.htm
www.learning-theories.com/experiential-learning-kolb.html

Lulu
www.lulu.com/gb/en

Mind-mapping
www.buzan.org
www.mindjet.com
www.publishedandprofitable.com

Natalie Goldberg's techniques
www.nataliegoldberg.com

National Association of Writers in Education
www.nawe.co.uk/the-writers-compass.html

National Novel Writing Month
www.nanowrimo.org

Scrivener writing programme
www.literatureandlatte.com

Second Life
http://secondlife.com

Writing 'morning pages'
www.750words.com

References

Allison, D., *Bastard out of Carolina* (New York: Plume/ Dutton Signet, Penguin, 1992).

Brande, D., *Becoming a writer* (London: Macmillan, 1996).

Call, W. and Kramer, M. (eds.), *Telling true stories: a non-fiction writers' guide* (New York: Plume, 2007).

Cameron, J., *The artist's way* (London: Pan Macmillan, 1995).

Carver, R., 'On writing', *Fires: essays, poems, stories* (London: Collins Harvill, 1985).

—*Collected stories* (New York: The Library of America, 2009).

—*What we talk about when we talk about love* (New York: Alfred A. Knopf, 1981).

Ellis, B. E., *American psycho* (London: Picador, 1991).

Fenza, D. W., 'Creative writing and its discontents', *The Writer's Chronicle*, March/April 2000. Available online at: www.awpwriter.org/library/writers_chronicle_view/1697 (accessed 7 February 2013).

Flaubert, G., *Madame Bovary*, M. Cohen (ed.), E. M. Averling and P. De Man (trans.), 2nd edn (New York: Norton Critical Edition, 2005).

Glazner, Gary Mex, *How to make a living as a poet* (New York: Soft Skull Press, 2005).
Goldberg, N., *Writing down the bones* (Boston, Mass.: Shambhala, 2005).
Golding, W., *Lord of the flies* (London: Faber and Faber, 1954).
Goldman, W., *Adventures in the screen trade* (London: Abacus, 1996).
Hunt C. and Sampson F., *Writing: self and reflexivity* (Basingstoke: Palgrave Macmillan, 2006).
Internet World Stats. Available online at www.internetworldstats.com/stats/htm (accessed 7 February 2013).
Johnson, C., *Oxherding tale* (New York: Scribner, 2005).
Joyce, J., *Ulysses* (Paris: Sylvia Beach, 1922).
Kane, T. S., *The new Oxford guide to writing* (Oxford: Oxford University Press, 1994).
King, S., *On writing* (London: Hodder & Stoughton, 2001).
Kolb, D., *Experiential learning: experience as the source of learning and development* (Englewood Cliffs, NJ: Prentice-Hall, 1984).
Mamet, D., *A whore's profession* (London: Faber and Faber, 1994).
McKee, R., *Story: substance, structure, style and the principles of screenwriting* (London: Methuen Film Classics, 1999).
Milliot, J., 'Self-published titles topped 764,000 in 2009 as traditional output dipped', *Publishers' Weekly*, 14 April 2010. Available online at: www.publishersweekly.com/pw/by-topic/industry-news/publishing-and-marketing/article/42826-

self-published-titles-topped-764-000-in-2009-as-traditional-output-dipped.html (accessed 7 February 2013).

Page, B., 'E-book growth "reducing value"', *The Bookseller*, 29 March 2012. Available online at: www.thebookseller.com/news/e-book-growth-%e2%80%98reducing-value%e2%80%99.html (accessed 7 February 2013).

Palumbo, D., *Writing from the inside out* (New York: Wiley, 2000).

Qualley, D., *Turns of thought: teaching composition as reflexive inquiry* (London: Heinemann, 1997).

Rushdie, S., *Midnight's children* (London: Jonathan Cape, 1981).

Schultz, J., *Writing from start to finish* (Portsmouth, NH: Boynton/Cook Publishers/Heinemann, 2005).

Tolkien, J. R. R., *The hobbit* (London: George Allen & Unwin, 1937).

—*The lord of the rings* (London: George Allen & Unwin, 1954).

Tolstoy, L. N., *War and peace*, trans. R. Edmonds (Harmondsworth: Penguin, 1974).

Woods, D., 'You need a good attitude, not a good degree, says Ernst & Young' *HR Magazine*, 13 February 2012.

Writer's market (Ohio: F+W Media, 2012).

Writer's & artists' yearbook 2013 (London: Bloomsbury, 2012).

Index

Allison, Dorothy 28–29
assessment 144–64
  degree classification
    152–53
  examiners 155–56
  feedback 152, 163–64
  formative
    assessment 144–47
  markers 156–60
  process 152–64
  summative assessment
    144, 147–52
  using 164
assignment tools 77

Bastard out of Carolina
  28–29, 32–34
  beginning of novel 29
  'Bone' 28–29
  mini scenes 32–34
  'model telling',
    and 32–33
  quick pace of 29
  bibliography 161

Cameron, Julia 42–43
Carver, Raymond 89

Chisholm, Ally 7–19
clustering 44
Comma Press 109
composting 40–41
Connor, Rachel 120–22
Cooper Clarke, John 110
creative writing degree
  benefits 2–5
  expectations
    see expectations
  preparing to study 6
  time of uncertainty,
    and 2
critical reflective
  essay 124–43
  background 125–26
  dealing with
    difficulties 136–40
  demystification of 133–35
  differences from academic
    essay 133–35
  reflective/reflexive
    activity, as 127–28
  'string to your bow' 126
  tradition 126
  types 128
  writing 140–43

Index

diary writing 46–47
discussion forums 76–77

editing 87–104
  amount of 88–89
  Joyce, James 89–90
  myth of the finished
    story 87–88
  shared activity 91–96
  summative editing
    100–4
  technique 90–91
  Tolkien, J. R. R., and 89
  'trusted reader' 92
Ellis, Brett Easton 13
expectations 1–5
  benefits of 2
  'life lessons' 4–5
  Norris, Sharon 1–6
  practical advice 5
  practical skills of 3–4
  self-discovery and
    development 3
  Shiflett, Shawn 1
  time of uncertainty 2

Facebook 171–73
Faulkner, William 22
Fergusson, Lorna 37–54
Flaubert, Gustave 24–25
free-writing 41–43
  Cameron, Julia 42–43

daily writing 43
definition of 41–42
'morning pages' 42
reviewing 43
Freud, Sigmund 127

Goldman, William 12
graduation 165–81
  blogs 171–73
  career paths 180–81
  day jobs 178–79
  finding an agent and
    publisher 175–77
  getting published
    online 171–73
  local scene 175
  networking 166–69
  online
    communities 173–75
  preparation 165–66
  raw talent, myth
    of 169–71
  self-publishing 177–78
  staying motivated 178–79
Green, Michelle 113–16

Harvard University 55
Hocking, Amanda 177–78

Jameel, Nabila 105–23
Johnson, Charles 26–28
Jordan, Spencer 127–28

journaling 45–47
  combining with writing skills 46
  diary, difference from 46
  emotions of 47
Joyce, James 89–90

Kalu, Peter 116–17
Kidd, Helen 144–64
King, Stephen 12
Kolb, David 125

live chats 77

Madame Bovary 24–26, 35
  empathy 25–26
  first sentence 24
  images in 25
  timeline management 35
Mamet, David 14
McKee, Rob 14
Mellor, Ben 117–20
mind-mapping 44
morning pages 42

National Association of Writers 168
National Novel Writing Month (NaNoWriMo) 174–75
Norris, Sharon 124–43

noting 47–49
  digital recorder, and 48
  notebooks, and 48
  scraps of paper, and 48–49
  Scrivener, and 49

online learning 71–86
  attention 85–86
  basic ideas 84–85
  creative writing, and 71
  invisibility online 79–81
  lack of immediacy 72
  language and structure matters 82–84
  orientation, and 74–75
  practising craft 81–82
  pros and cons of 72–73
  questions 75–76
  tools and resources 76–79
  virtual learning environment (VLE) 73–75
O'Reilly, Sally 165–81
Oxherding 26–28, 34
  dates as time-markers 34
  first sentence 26–27
  opening chapter 27–28

pre-writing 37–54
  definition of 37
  downside of 53–54

pre-writing (*cont.*)
  reasons for 37–38
  tools and techniques of 39–52
preparations 6

reading 20–36
  list of questions 22–29
  making your own list 29–31
  'post-dramatic flashbacks' 21
  reading differently to other readers 20–22
reading aloud 105–23
  audio-visual 108–9
  body language 106–8
  Connor, Rachel 120–22
  getting work out there 122–23
  Green, Michelle 113–16
  Kalu, Peter 116–17
  Mellor, Ben 117–20
  performance types 108–12
  Royle, Nicholas 113
  voice 106
redrafting 87–104
  see also editing
Reeder, Elizabeth 71–86
research 50–51
Royle, Nicholas 113

Schultz, John 32
Scrivener 49
skills 7–19
  attention to detail 17–18
  ideas 15
  memorable use of language 11–13
  organisation 13–15
  planning 14–15
  power of description 9–11
  reading as a writer 8–9
  research skills 15–16
  structure 14
  willingness to learn 7–8
smaller presses 177

thinking 39–40
Tolkien, J. R. R. 89
Tolstoy, Leo 20
Twitter 171–73

virtual learning environment (VLE) 73–75

webinars 79
wikis 79
Woolf, Virginia 21
workshops 55–70
  approaches, and 60–61
  attending, and 63

collegiate relationship 57
content, and 58
criticism, and 56
definition of 56
emotions, and 61
famous writers, and 55
feedback, and
  61–62, 67–69
genres,
  difference in 63–64
Harvard University 55
importance of 70
improvement of
  work, and 59
own work 59–63
personal attacks 66–67
post-university 69–70
preparation 64–65
questions and suggestions
  65–66
social media, and 62–63
structure 56–59
*Writers' & artists'
  yearbook* 176

X-Factor, The 178

Young, Jennifer 55–70